The Life
and Loves
of BONNEY LOPEZ

An Inspiring Story of Determination and Faith

By Bonifacio Lopez

Publisher
B.A. Lopez & Associates
789 Sherman Street, Suite 440
Denver, Colorado 80203

Third Printing
June 2003

ISBN 0-9725641-0-1

Table Of Contents

Table Of Contents (cont)

DEDICATION

First and foremost, I dedicate this book to my late, beloved wife, Lucille Marquez Lopez. She was and is the great love of my life-her spirit remains with me; unquestionably ordained to intertwine with mine throughout eternity.

I also dedicate this book to my children-all of whom are college graduates and products of *mi gente*, from the San Luis Valley. My children are: Micheal Bonney Lopez, a successful and adept business executive; James Joseph Lopez, M.D., a skilled and knowledgeable physician; Ronald Albert Lopez, an experienced and consummate police detective; and lastly, the only daughter any man would ever need, Jilda Mari Lopez, a scholarly and gifted bank vice-president.

I also dedicate this book to the many Latinos who were and are to be-from doctors and lawyers to college presidents, teachers, U.S. ambassadors and the hard-working Latinos who continue to give and expect nothing in return... and many more, especially those who have come from the great San Luis Valley of Colorado.

The Lopez Family, 1960
Lucille and Bonney
Micheal, Jilda, Ronald and James

AUTHOR'S FORWARD

I've considered writing this story for over thirty years but it wasn't until after my son, Micheal, died that I decided it was time. He always wanted to know more about his family and had begun making a record of stories told him by his grandpa Albert. Before his death, he asked that I make a record of my life so that his children might have a better understanding of their ancestors and where they came from. At first I thought of doing a genealogy study but then I decided against it. My story would take less time and would be much easier to write.

My desire was to name all the people who took this journey with me. If I have excluded anyone, it is not because they are not valued or did not have an impact in my life. On the contrary, my testimony is an affirmation of fact in their behalf. I realize that when I tell these stories and say peoples' names, I have kept even the most forgotten, obscure person now buried in an unmarked grave alive.

I must mention, in particular, my good friend Tomas Romero-a professional writer who struggled with me, at the start, to make this book possible.

Every time I visit *el valle*-the San Luis Valley: San

Antonio, Antonito and Cenicero, I re-live the experiences of my childhood. Not only do I experience the lives of *mi gente* (my people) in my memory, but I actually visualize friends, former classmates and relatives still living in that unchanging place called the San Luis Valley.

In *"El Valle"* "I see people I love, essentially existing in a manner reminiscent of sixty or one hundred and sixty years ago. They seem to be the same people living on the same land, enduring the same floods amidst the same surroundings. Some may view this as a negative condition. I do not.

I once asked a Zuni Indian why so many young Indians do not leave the reservation. He replied: "We do leave and we get the white man's education. Then we return and live like Indians, just like the white man wants us to do."

Not much has changed in *el valle*. Not many leave their *condition* except for those who intentionally or simply by fortuitous chance, receive a formal education. There is no straight line to anyone's vision or dream. I'm living proof of that. Mine is an unscripted story of a blessed and lucky man.

I am an unconventional type of man, who has stumbled at times, but somehow I've still managed to move forward and survive many trials and tests of stamina and faith. Eventually, I thrived in one of the world's wealthiest and most celebrated countries.

Still, mine is a small-town American story, with which a person from any background, heritage or creed could find a common experience. From an outsider's perspective, the San Luis Valley was like a foreign country-relatively unchanged in her people and their customs.

All the same, I've always been aware of my roots and of my ties to *el valle* even as my eyes opened to a world I never knew existed.

Along the continuum of my life, various people and events have interposed themselves upon me. These events and people have been an amalgamation of brief or extended encounters; endowed with harsh or gentle features or filled with great sadness or joy.

Still others, like my wife, Lucille, have maintained a constancy throughout my life. Her spirit, energy and fortitude is forever with me, even after her death. As a result, what I wish to do is draw and establish a connection from the past through the present and on to the future.

I trust that this book will be read by my immediate family as well as *mi gente* in both Conejos and Costilla counties in Colorado. I hope that they would encourage their children's children to stay in school so that they would be afforded the many opportunities available to all Spanish-Americans, and not just to those Spanish-Americans who live in urban communities. In rural communities such as the San Luis Valley, Spanish-Americans know who they are but do not experience the same golden opportunities (especially in terms of education) afforded to los *gabachos (the white man)*.

If Anastacio and Delfina Jiron (my maternal grandparents) and if Luis and Sarah Lopez (my paternal grandparents) were able to do it for Alberto and Sarah Lopez (my parents). They in turn did it for me-Bonifacio Alberto Lopez (Bonney). So can all San Luis Valley parents and grandparents do the same for their children.

TO MY CHILDREN'S CHILDREN

I am not familiar with all the particulars of both my parents' lives. Moreover, there is much about Lucille and I that my children, Jilda and Ronald, do not know. There is also a great deal about my son, Micheal that his children do not know. Additionally, my grandchildren have little knowledge of their deceased Uncle Jimmy. I would like my grandchildren-Joelle, Gabriel, Joshua and Jennifer and their children's children to acknowledge and to appreciate *nuestra familia*. They deserve to know all there is to know about our family. Thus, I had better write my story.

My story will be about my early life, young adulthood and my wonderful marriage to Lucille Marquez

My father and mother, Sarah and Alberto Lopez, on their wedding day. Cenicero, Colorado August 1930

Lopez. This record will include times before my grandchildren were born and after I became their grandpa.

As I have begun to record *mis memorias* (my memories), I again realize that my father and mother led truly good and worthwhile lives. They were both born in humble adobe homes, delivered by midwives, the local newspapers carrying no notice of their births. Their own thoughts were never recorded, whatever they might have been. All the footsteps they took never left a mark.

Rather, the mark came through their children's steps, which they conceived and nurtured with generous love. Their epitaph might have read: Alberto and Sarah bore children and one of their sons, Bonney, in turn, had his own family, with three fine sons and a lovely daughter.

I would hope that when this story is concluded, the readers would feel that my life too, was good and worthwhile. I wish to be remembered, not for the goods and glory I have collected, but for the good I have done in my life.

My father and mother at their home in Alamosa, all dressed up to go to a party. Summer of 1956

The village where I was born-Lobatos, also known as Cenicero by some former residents, is not really a village anymore. It is located three miles east of Antonito, Colorado in the south-central part of *El Valle de San Luis* (San Luis Valley). For all intents and purposes, one could say it is a ghost town. Lobatos lies in a bend near an *acequia* (a large ditch) where cottonwoods grow thick and sage-covered plains roll away and climb higher and higher towards the mountains. This tiny hamlet of an agriculture-based *pueblito* (small town) seems protected... even lost.

I was born in this quiet place; delivered in my grandmother's home on June 2, 1931. The thick-walled adobe home where my abuelos lived was made with a mixture of mud, straw and animal droppings. It has long since been reduced by rain and wind to what it was in the beginning-ordinary soil.

Some may be surprised that I find no sadness or remorse in the change and deterioration that has taken place there. Indeed, this is simply a reinforcement of my spirit-an affirmation of what once was, will always be.

Only the form of anything, not the substance, ever really changes. Bodies and buildings are made to change and deteriorate or to eventually die and crumble.

That which remains, our memories, is most important. As long as we pass our stories down to our sons and our daughters, repeating the names of *la gente*, the people from this part of *el valle* will live forever.

When you combine a "close-to-us-in-blood (*en sangre)*"

mettle with a Catholic/Hispanic faith in a hereafter, you can see why we fear death less than those who are not as tied to the land. I believe that it is nearly impossible to be a farmer and lack faith in God. Imagine the faith that it takes to place a seed in dry, barren ground where it is almost impossible to extract any living plant with the expectation that it will grow. A farmer's faith knows, without a doubt, that the seed that was planted will reap an abundant harvest.

Retired Adams county schoolteacher, Procopio Jiron, who is a second cousin on my mother Sarah (Jiron) Lopez's side, has written about Cenicero with great passion and understanding. Jiron, like myself, was born in Cenicero-a lovely place to be from and one of the most beautiful places on earth.

In a 1988 article for *Colorado Heritage Magazine*, Senor Jiron reveals how the name Cenicero (meaning "pile of ashes" in Spanish) was derived from the fine dust emanating from the hills some eight miles southwest of the village. According to Procopio, as oxen-drawn covered wagons moved goods from Taos, New Mexico to these isolated regions, the sharp hooves of the animals raised a fine sand that was blown by winds to the base of the neighboring hills. Jiron describes an almost idyllic lifestyle in el *valle*. Sr. Jiron speaks of summer grasses growing as high as a horse's belly, where flocks of sheep and herds of cattle and horses were allowed to graze on an open range. Water was plentiful and as a result, the crops were abundant.

Then came events, which were so entertainingly and

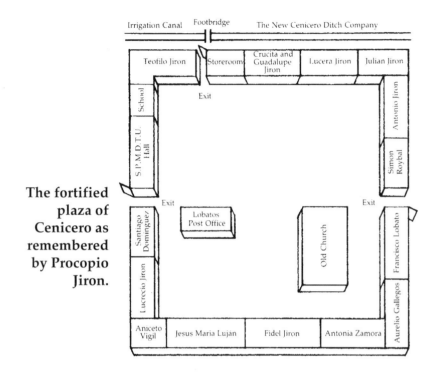

The fortified plaza of Cenicero as remembered by Procopio Jiron.

bitter sweetly depicted in the *Milagro Beanfield War* novel (and movie by the same name). Centuries old rights to water usage were lost, stolen or bought at criminally unfair prices by opportunists and entrepreneurial exploiters. Irrigation ditches which once overflowed now were mere trickles of what they were. Our grandmother's garden dried up. Fruit trees no longer produced apples. Men were forced to abandon the land and find work in the mines and as sheepherders in faraway states. Land was fenced off and those who remained lived on small tracts of land that were far too small to produce sufficient crops to survive. From an economic standpoint, residents derived more from government assistance than they contributed in terms of taxes or products.

Presently, what is conspicuously clear is that *Cenicero (and San Antonio)* is no place for the young or anyone in search of opportunity. The post office is gone and so too, is the *tiendita* (grocery store). Yet, once or twice a month the bell still peals and resonates at the tiny, well-maintained *Iglesia de La Sagrada Familia* (Church of the Holy Family). Mass is said in Spanish and elderly women who modestly cover their heads with mantillas accept the communion host on their tongues.

Rendering of the first church built in southern Colorado in 1854 at Guadalupe.

La Iglesia de la Sagrada Familia, rebuilt in 1952, still celebrates mass.

Occasionally an urban cousin or grandchild will come to help bury an elder in a 200 year-old family plot but for the most part this is a place for recollections and not for expectations to flourish.

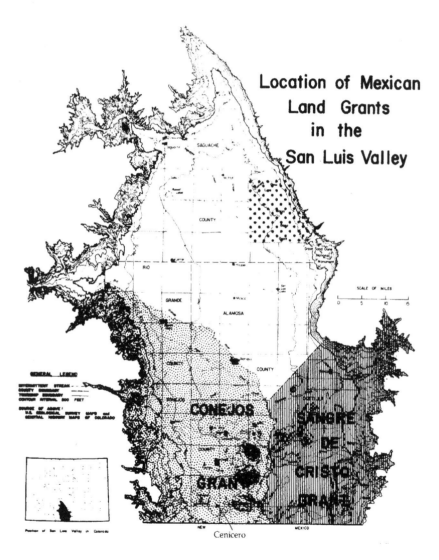

Location of Mexican
Land Grants
in the
San Luis Valley

LIFE IN EL VALLE

For the first few years of my life I lived with my family in nearby San Antonio, where I attended grade school from the first through the sixth grades. Those were innocent, happy times; some could even say almost blissfully happy, given the state of our universe today.

We lived next door to my Mama Sarah, my paternal grandmother. What a delightful person! I don't know how much formal education she had but she was intelligent, wise and very well read. If you wanted to know something, you asked grandma. She had all the answers. She was always reading, it seemed. She could read the Denver Post out loud, translating from English to Spanish as she read. It was truly amazing.

Grandpa Luis Lopez, Cousin Bobby Quintana and Grandma Sarah Lopez. Visiting Cousin Bobby at his home in California, 1955. Note Grandma holding her "roll your own" cigarette.

I can still picture her sitting in her favorite chair, in the kitchen, "directing traffic." She was a heavy-set woman who rolled her own cigarettes. No one ever questioned her authority. She was like "The Godmother." If you said the wrong thing or made a move that was offensive to any adult, she would dress you down with just a couple of words (*"Mal ayen tus juevos"*), causing terrific embarrassment. Notwithstanding these occasional blows, we loved her dearly.

Whenever we were going away for a period of time, we would kneel before her and grandpa to receive their *bendición*-blessing. Parents, uncles, aunts and cousins all received her blessings. If you stayed with them overnight, you'd plan on dinner at 4:00 p.m., helping with the dishes, then kneeling around grandma to say the rosary. Grandma Sarah couldn't kneel so she would stay in her chair. It seemed like that rosary would go on for hours. We would be in bed by 8:30 p.m. and then up again for breakfast by 5:00 a.m. the next morning.

In the spring and summer months, grandma would bake bread outside in the *horno* (adobe oven/

Bonney standing by *el horno* at Navajo Indian Reservation in Taos, New Mexico, 1990.

outdoor wood burning stove). The preparations, for the baking experience was one to remember. Grandma would first go out and sweep out the inside of the *horno* to make sure it was perfectly clean. Then she'd build a fire inside. There was an opening in front and another on top of the adobe mud horno. The one opening was used to slide the bread into and work with it. The top opening was to let the smoke out and help the fire burn hotter.

Grandma would then proceed to make the wonderful loaves. She didn't use a bowl; the large kitchen table was all she needed. She moved the flour into a circle and put all of the other ingredients in the middle. And then she began to knead. Watching her you could see the muscles in her hands, arms and back moving with great strength. In no time she had several loaves ready for baking.

Once the *horno* was hot enough (I often wondered how she knew when it was ready), grandma would sweep out the brazas (hot ashes) and cover both openings with wooden covers and wet cloths to keep the heat from escaping. She then slid her loaves into the oven. Later, just as mysteriously, she would come to take the bread out of the oven. She would get busy doing something else and then all of a sudden she'd holler: "Let's take that bread out of the oven." I expected to see something akin to a chunk of coal. The loaves were golden brown and the aroma filled the air and made us hungry instantly. When we finally were able to have a slice it was light and airy and melted in our mouths. I get hungry every time I think about it.

I was a child of the depression and I remember not having many things. A dime seemed like a fortune to me, yet I never felt impoverished. My entire family worked, from the littlest to the oldest. During harvest time, we'd load the whole family on a crew leader's truck and go pick peas, potatoes or other crops on neighboring farms. My infant sister, Gloria, would be placed in a shady spot and my mother, Sarah, would join the rest of us on mud-caked knees.

My father, Alberto, was fortunate to find on and off work with the WPA (Work Progress Administration). He would work for a month building national park facilities and then return home for another month. At other times, he worked

Eddie, Gloria and Bonney at Grandma Sarah's home in San Antonio, 1940.

Eddie at Grandpa Luis and Grandma Sara's grave in Otriz, Colorado, December 2001.

as a sheepherder. For six months we lived in Leadville, Colorado. My father found work there; helping to build Camp Hale, home of the celebrated World War II 10th Mountain Army Division. This meant that my family had to share a small apartment with another family. It was so cramped we had to sleep in shifts.

During the summer months, like many children of this era, I lived with my maternal grandparents, Anastacio and Delfina Jiron, in Cenicero. This, however, was not because my own parents had abandoned me. This was a cultural/ familial custom. Even at a young age, I was expected to be of service and useful. What better place to be of service than to live at the home of my own grandparents. While living with them during the summer, I could do useful household chores such as cutting firewood, gardening, milking cows and assisting with the tending of their small flock of sheep.

I remember beautiful scenes when water was plentiful and grandpa would take me along to cut wild hay on his property, just about a mile east of his home. Grandma would bring us lunch and we'd enjoy what I considered a "picnic" in the tall grass and shade of a cottonwood tree. That evening, after supper, the three of us would sit on discarded buggy seats, in the back yard, enjoying the bright stars and burning *bunigas* (cow pies) to fend off mosquitoes.

As I understand, Grandpa's home (farm) is located within the boundaries of the Conejos Land Grant. Settlers first came to this area in the mid eighteen hundreds. Among them was Jose Guadalupe Jiron, Grandpa Anastacio's grandfather. At age thirty, Padre Guadalupe traveled from Peña Blanca New Mexico and settled in Cenicero (land surrounding the San Antonio River), shortly after the signing of the Treaty of Guadalupe Hidalgo in 1848. I've read he was an expert horseman and buffalo hunter.

I've also read that Great Great Grandfather Guadalupe ("Padre Lupe") became very wealthy. At his death, he left each of his six children 800 head of sheep, 80 head of cattle, 160 acres of cultivated land, as well as money and gold. I guess none of this wealth dribbled down far enough because I don't remember my mother inheriting anything from her parents.

Grandma Delfina (Mondragon) Jiron had two brothers, Roman and Celedonio Mondragon. Both were very well

known goldsmiths in and around Santa Fe. Their superior quality jewelry was unmatched and considered the best at the time.

Grandpa Anastacio and Grandma Delfina ("Fina") in the front yard of their home in Cenicero, early 1950s

15

On November 26, 1900 Celedonio gathered six other men at his home and founded the S.P.M.D.T.U. (Sociedad Protección Mutua De Trabajadores Unidos—Translated as "Mutual Protective Society for United Workers"). Among the seven men was Juan Antonio Marquez, an ancestor of Lucille Marquez, my wife.

The S.P.M.D.T.U., headquartered in Antonito Colorado, still has chapters throughout Colorado and New Mexico. During the late 1800s and early 1900s large numbers of workers were injured or killed in dangerous construction or mining jobs, leaving behind widows and children unable to provide for themselves. The "Society" was established to

Statue of Celedonio Mondragon unveiled and placed on the south side of the *Concilio Superior* (Superior Council) building in Antonito, Colorado, on September 2, 2000.

1900 Concilio Superior Antonito, Colorado, erected in early nineteen hundreds.

assist with medical, burial, food and clothing to the worker's survivors. I was present when a delegation of the Society officers come to my grandparents' home to present my grandma Delfina with a $1,000 check when grandpa Anastacio died.

A Centennial Celebration was held on September 2, 2000 honoring Sr. Celedonio Mondragon. A life-size bronze statute of Celedonio was unveiled and stands outside the building (main chapter) in Antonito, Colorado.

Public swimming pools were unheard of in the 1930s when I lived in the valley. The only places available to swim were large irrigation ditches or the rivers. Spring thaws always brought about flooding of the San Antonio River, located not too far from home.

It seemed like every evening my parents would take us

Picture of Grandma Delfina Jiron which appeared in the Alamosa Courier Daily Newpaper in 1947 with a front page story about original settlers in the San Luis Valley. It was an old custom to wear black *"luto"*during time of grieving for a deceased loved one. Grandma "Fina" once told me she started wearing black when her mother died. I never knew her to wear anything but black. She'd buy new outfits but they all looked the same.

to watch the flood waters overrunning the river banks… carrying off small bridges, trees, livestock and debris. For us, this was a form of entertainment, just like going to a carnival or circus. "Never go near the river; people drown easily," parents would warn their children. Naturally, we feared the river.

I recall "swimming" in the nearby irrigation ditch. We called it "swimming" but none of us really knew how to swim. The water was only 2-3 feet deep, so it was more like wading.

One sunny summer afternoon my cousin, Efrim Jiron, and I decided to sneak off to the San Antonio River. By this time (mid-June) flooding was over. The water was warmer, clear and you could see the trout swimming around. We found large tree limbs hanging over the water. Underneath the limbs were large; not too deep wading water holes… perfect for swimming, we thought. We disrobed, walked on the limb and jumped in. Ma a a n! What a shock, not from the cold water but from the bottomless hole. Suddenly, my feet touch the bottom and I realize I didn't drown. This was only the first of many near drowning experiences. We stayed there the rest of the day, until we learned to swim. After that we'd sneak off at every opportunity until one day my tío Filandro (Efrim's father) caught us.

"Don't you realize you shouldn't get in the water until *el día de San Juan* (June 24th, St. John's day)?" Grandma would say. "And you wet your forehead first, before getting in the water. *Pídele a Dios que no te pique la agua.* (Ask God that you don't get stung by the water)", she'd say.

Springtime was not only lambing time (birthing time) but also *la trasquila* (sheering time - clipping the sheep's wool). Grandpa Anastacio, my uncles and neighbors would spend days (sometimes weeks) sheering in the shade of the adobe garage, one ewe (sheep) at a time.

Hand held clippers used for sheering looked much like a large pair of scissors. It was not unusual to see the clippers accidentally cut into the ewes' skin and cause bleeding. A bottle of kerosene was readily available to use as a disinfectant and to help stop the bleeding.

Wool was packed into huge burlap sacks, loaded unto a horse driven wagon (two sacks on each wagon) and delivered to Antonito. I have no idea how much money Grandpa received from the sale of wool, but I do remember it being a very important source of income.

We enjoyed similar experiences at "thrashing time" in the fall, when the neighbors would gather to help grandpa with the wheat harvest. The huge thrashing machine was powered by a fifteen-foot long, twelve-inch wide belt attached to a large spool on a tractor. The tractor didn't move but its engine ran all day. The belt just hung on there between the thrashing machine and the tractor. I could never figure out why it didn't slip off. And the noise... it was so loud... we couldn't hear each other talk. This machine simply separated the wheat from the chaff (straw). It would take several men to feed the bales into the machine and handle the full sacks as the grain came out the other side. Again, the grain would be loaded unto wagons and sold in Antonito. Grandma and the other women, of course, were responsible for feeding the twelve to fifteen men sitting around the large kitchen table at noontime.

Sunday was always a special day of rest and worship. No one worked on Sunday, except maybe those responsible for feeding the animals and milking the cows, early morning. Most of the work we did on Saturday was in preparation for the Sunday holiday. We spent the day preparing meals for Sunday, pressing and washing our Sunday clothes, taking Saturday night baths, getting the wagon ready and getting feed ready for the horses.

Before sunup on Sunday morning, we'd load up the wagon and head for Our Lady of Guadalupe church in Conejos, about five miles away. We'd all be fasting… no breakfast because we were to take Holy Communion, and, "You don't eat or drink before taking the body and blood of Christ," grandma would tell us.

We often arrived about two hours before Mass. Grandpa always wanted to be there early so he could spend time socializing with friends and neighbors out in front of the church. Grandma would take me in the church with her. We'd sit alone in the very front pew. She'd pray the rosary, than she'd pray her memorized prayers out loud, then she'd pray the rosary again. She'd just pray and pray and pray. I'd get tired and sneak out to listen to the men outside. That didn't last because within minutes, grandpa would send me back in. By this time there were a few more people sitting in the pews. Just before mass began, the men started walking in, one or two at a time.

The first ten or fifteen pews on both sides of the isle were reserved for what I assume were well to do or important parishioners. Grandpa must have been "well to do" or "important," because he paid a monthly (or annual) stipend for the use of the very front pew in that church. He never worried about someone taking his seat. Maybe that's why he waited 'til the last minute to come in.

The words "Numero Uno" "The Anastacio Jiron Family"

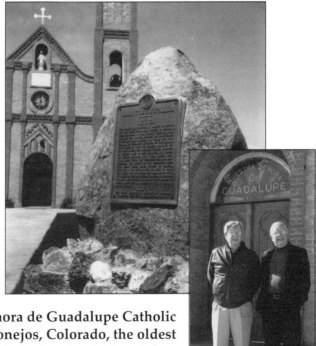

Bonney and Eddie in front of Nuestra Senora de Guadalupe Catholic Church in Conejos, Colorado, the oldest church in Colorado. Picture taken December 2001.

appeared on a small bronze plaque placed on each side of the pew. To this day, the "Anastacio Jiron Family" name still appears on one of the large beautifully stained glass windows of this historic church.

You don't hear it much nowadays, but in the old days you always heard women talk about "spring cleaning". At Grandma's home it was more than just spring cleaning. It was a three-month long project. It seemed that cleaning house was all they did all summer.

First, grandma would put in a new dirt floor in *la cocinita* (small porch). On her knees, by hand she'd spread a mixture of mud and straw to level out the uneven, worn down floor. When she was finished, the new dried floor appeared like freshly poured concrete.

Next she and one or two other women would take down *mantas* (white cheesecloth) covering the ceilings in every room of the house. They'd wash the mantas and tack them back up. Then they'd go about white washing the walls.

Finally, they'd take down the beds, wash sheets (pillowcases) and refill mattresses with cotton, if necessary. Than the fun work began.

The *cobijas* (blankets) had to be washed outside, in the ditch. This venture could take two or three days, depending on how many neighbors wanted to join and make it a community blanket wash day.

First we'd lay a twelve-foot long, 12-inch wide plank across the ten-foot wide ditch. The water was crystal clear and about two to three feet deep. Sometimes we'd place two or three planks so two women could work together on each plank.

The blanket first was dipped in the water so it was completely wet. One end was placed on the plank and the rest of the blanket floated downstream in the water. While this was going on, the younger kids would stand on the blanket being washed to help keep it from being carried away by the fast flowing water.

Using homemade soap and a brush the women would scrub one foot of the blanket at a time, then pull the next section another foot and scrub that one. As they completed each section, it dropped into the clear water under the plank and started rinsing. When the one side was finished, they'd flip the blanket over and do the same to the backside. After both sides were done, we'd help wring the water from the *cobija*, hang it on a nearby fence and let it dry in the sun.

An elaborate *compadre* and *padrino* system existed, where a child can have multiple sets of godparents. Some believe this system existed, some think, because of a predominately Catholic upbringing. It became a common practice because it enhanced your chances of survival. Many others in the same village would assume moral responsibility for your care-a sort of "I am my brother's keeper" philosophy.

It was my grandmother Delfina's ambition that I become a store clerk. In her view, wearing a tie and starched collar shirt was the height of success. I offer this anecdote not for amusement, but as an illustration of how far we have come. My grandmother saw her father, husband and sons wear out the knees on their trousers by doing hard labor. However, my uncle Alcario and my mother were able to go college and become teachers. Both taught grade school in surrounding rural communities. Grandmother Delfina wanted only the very best for me. In her limited, but sadly accurate view of the world, the most a young Spanish-American boy could aspire to was a job such as this.

However, it was this same humble woman who gave me my first fifty dollars when I announced that I was going to college. "Here, *hito*, take this," she said as she unwrapped a tightly knotted bandana and handed me her hard-earned money. Only God knows how many years of sacrifice it took her to accrue this small fortune-dime by dime, nickel by nickel. She acquired this money by selling eggs and *queso* (milk cheese cakes).

Like their ancestors before them, my parents and grandparents lived lives that were quite pastoral in nature. They tended to their small herds of sheep, cattle and crops on a daily basis. The land they tilled was rock laden, lacking in nutrients, harsh and unforgiving-difficult to plow and even more difficult from which to force fruit. What was bountiful was perseverance and courage, not our harvests.

There was less of everything, especially water and other natural resources. Over centuries and through trial and error, a successful strategy for survival and a pattern for living evolved among those in *el valle*. My ancestors learned how to adapt and work with the environment, rather than continuously fighting nature. No towering forests exist in the southwest. Precious pinewood and other difficult to find hardwood were in demand for heating and furniture making.

The most abundant resource for building a home in *el valle* is the clay soil-one needs to make proper use of the dirt you stand on by turning it into adobe bricks. I remember helping my father make adobes to build our home. We mixed straw, dirt and water and poured it into forms, making two adobes at a time. We then laid them out in the sun to dry, covering them at night in case of rain. After making several thousand adobes, we began to build our home.

There are two characteristics, which have defined northern New Mexico and southern Colorado Hispanic/ Spanish colonial life for centuries: scarcity and cooperation. For example, the Arabic inspired *acequia* system of cooperative water use management made as much sense to my ancestors as it had to the indigenous Native Americans who also dealt with limited resources.

We built our thick adobe walled town centers with a large communal square. This made sense to us because the walls kept people in and others, such as attackers, out. Certainly, at the time we had no idea that newer immigrants from other parts of the nation would consider our towns so aesthetically pleasing. Who would have thought that something so decidedly practical could become the rage among the artsy, twentieth-century avant-garde types?

Hispanic Cultura

By habit, I trust people. I trust family, friends and all those who touch my life. I like to help those in need and am willing to endure occasional disappointment or material loss rather than suffer a greater, more painful consequence: loss of faith in another person.

These are some of my thousands of cultural "givens" or historically validated understandings about what I have expected from others and from what I expect of myself. For example, I can walk into a pool hall or public place, exchange an "orale *ese*" ("What's going on?") gaze with a total stranger. Just by a nod of a head, we indicate whether or not we want to engage one another-be it in casual conversation, conflict or seduction. Life, to me, in so many ways, is as predictable as it was for my ancestors who lived in a so-called uncomplicated "peasant" culture. In effect, I am a seventeenth century southwestern *anciano* (old man) in a 21st century business suit.

My story here has much in common with the life experience of other Latinos. Yet, I distinguish myself somewhat from men of my own generation. As much as I love my community and happily feel a part of a greater whole; I am also an entrepreneur, a risk-taker, and when I have to, capable of going it alone. In this manner, I differ from most of my childhood friends. Call me a capitalist if you must and wish, but I hasten to add that I am a compassionate one.

Envidia (jealousy), a trait which folklore says permeates our culture, has always been offered as an excuse for not making individual social progress. The story of the lobsters in the bucket who continuously pull back a companion who tries to escape has been told so many times within our culture that we now accept it as truth. As the argument goes, we had to learn how to cooperate during times of adversity and limited resources. Unfortunately, any person striking out on his own is viewed as a threat to the group.

I would like to dispel this myth. From my perspective, both personally and professionally, I have been witness to scores of acts of kindness and generosity by Latinos to accept this assertion as fact. Fellow Latinos businessmen have helped me enormously and I am willing to get in the trenches anytime to create more opportunities for *mi gente.*

I am a member of many professional organizations, but take greatest pride in being active in the Denver Hispanic Chamber of Commerce. I have a profound conviction about what it means to be an elder. If, in any manner, I can help a fledgling young Latino or Latina businessperson succeed or eliminate mistakes in their lives, then I intend to do so.

Traditions

When I was growing up, I participated in centuries old Hispanic traditions in San Antonio and in Cenicero with my grandparents. Sometimes I was just an onlooker and the adults were the ones having all the fun.

I remember the *"Dando Los Días"* (Giving/Singing the "days") tradition that was celebrated in Cenicero. A small group of men would start out early New Year's Eve at someone's home. Two or three of them would play musical instruments (guitar, violin, banjo, trumpet or perhaps harmonica), and all of them would sing. They didn't necessarily have great voices but they knew the words and could always improvise with a sense of humor.

The group would get larger as they picked up new participants from house to house. Sometimes they'd lose a few along the way, depending upon the amount of wine that was served at each house.

You never knew when they'd arrive at your home. It could be as early as 7 p.m. or maybe closer to midnight. Often, they'd show up around 2:00 a.m. Once, I remember they appeared at 7:00 a.m. We were having breakfast and thought that they had forgotten us. Boy, were we glad to see them.

These men would come to your door and begin singing. It didn't matter to them if there were any lights on at the house. Often we had already gone to bed, but they'd stand there and sing until someone opened the door and invited them in. According to Frank Amadeo White, who co-authored a booklet entitled "Dando Los Días," one of the most popular verses sung before entering a home was:

En el marco de esta puerta,	*At the threshold of this door,*
Pongo un pie, pongo dos pies,	*I place one foot, I place two,*
A todita esta gente,	*To all these people,*
Buenas noches les de Dios.	*May God grant a good night.*

Though we were in our pajamas, the men would come in and we would enjoy the festivities. Grandma and her helpers (my mother and aunts) would begin serving *biscochitos* (Mexican cookies), *empanaditas de carne* (rolled sweetmeats), *posole* and whatever other delicacies they'd prepared for this special occasion. Grandpa and his helpers would serve the coffee and wine, if they wanted wine. Most of them did. After an hour or so, depending upon how much fun everyone was having, the group would move on to the next home.

At exactly midnight, Junior (cousin Alcario Jiron, Jr.) and any other cousin spending the night with us, would bring in the New Year by ringing the large railroad bell, typically kept in grandpa's barn. We spent a good part of the previous week propping up this heavy bell for the best part of the ceremony, which lasted two or three minutes.

Another tradition that I recall occurred around

Christmas (December 28th). It was called *"El Día De Los Inocentes"* (The Day of the Innocents). I believe that this day is celebrated in the Catholic Church as a special holy day, but not in the sense that I remember it. To me, *El Día De Los Inocentes* was the day I would get up very early and confront as many people as possible before they caught on. It was just like April Fools Day, but instead you'd borrow something and not return it unless you were paid a ransom.

I recall one early morning going to Tía Ursulita's home to "borrow" a fresh loaf of bread so my mother could fix breakfast. As soon as she handed the bread to me, I said, *"Dios se lo page por inocente"* (May God repay you for being so innocent). I would not return that loaf of bread until my Tía paid me a quarter or gave me a piece of candy.

Another time (I must have been eight or nine) I went to Tía Rejina's (Grandpa Luis' sister) home around 6 a.m. and asked to borrow her car. She knew what I was up to and said I could borrow it, provided my father came by to pick it up. Of course, I changed my mind immediately… told her I didn't need it anyway. I didn't know how to drive.

On Christmas day, all of us kids would go house to house, in the neighborhood *"Pidiendo mis Christmas"* (asking for my Christmas gift). This tradition was similar to Halloween, except we didn't dress up in costumes and we went out in the daytime, never at night. No tricks, only treats… *empanaditas* and hard candy.

The Funeral

Funerals (family reunions) are always a sad time for those left behind, regardless of their culture. For us Hispanics the pain is the same, the grieving is the same, the loss is the same but the way we do all this seems a little different.

As we get older, we experience more funerals and sometimes we start looking forward to the next one. You see we know it's going to happen. We just don't know to whom or when but we know we're not getting out of this world alive. So why not make it as joyful as possible. After all death is a part of life—a celebration of our life on this earth. So we celebrate.

I've celebrated the life of my two children, my wife, my parents, my grandparents, great-grandparents, uncles, aunts, *primos*, amigos and so on. Each time the celebration is different.

In the old days we'd have the *velorio* (wake) at home. In the summer we'd make sure the body was kept in a cool room. The kitchen was full of *cocineras* (women friends and neighbors) who cooked day and night for family and friends who came to express their condolences (*dar el pésame*). Of course most would stick around for the meal, which sometimes was served around the clock. At night the penitents would come over to pray for the deceased and sing *alavaos* (Spanish Christian songs)-than pray some—than more singing—then eat again. Outside in the *dispensa* perhaps someone had brought wine or perhaps a bottle of whiskey for those who wished to participate.

I recall once walking over to a wake in the neighboring village with my parents. This was the third evening of the wake. We approached the home where the body lay in state. We could hear singing, praying and the commotion. Men were standing outside talking and laughing. As we got close we met with the son of the man in the casket and my father instead of offering condolences asked, "How are things going?" The son (a not so bright twenty-year-old) replied "*Ay como se está poniendo bueno*" (Say, it's really getting good). You hardly see this type of velorio (wake) any more.

My sister Gloria's day of Confirmation with Tía Ursulita in front of our home in Alamosa around 1948.

On March 2002 we celebrated the passing of my Uncle Fred Lopez, who died at age 94 in Pueblo, Colorado. The passing of Uncle Fred was the end of an era for me, as well as for my cousins at this family reunion. You see, my tío was the last of the Lopez family from whom I come. We were there to celebrate his passing with his two children, Eliu Lopez and Joan Lopez-Aguirre. The era for me started with my great grandfather, Juan Lopez. I knew Papa Juan Lopez. He had several sons whom I knew also. One of those sons was my grandfather Luis D. Lopez. Luis had several sons and daughters. Two of Grandpa Luis' sons were Alfredo (Fred) Lopez and Alberto (Albert, my father). Fred and Albert married two sisters, Ursulita (Uncle Fred's wife) and Sarah (Albert's wife and my mother). Albert & Sarah (my parents), Tía Ursulita and all the members on both sides of the family have died.

Uncle Fred was the last one. This was the end of an era for the Lopez family.

Uncle Fred and my father Alberto ("Mi Beto" as we called him) enjoying a toy buggy ride around their parents' home in San Antonio, Colorado, sometime between 1915 and 1918.

(Top row L-R) Alfredo Lopez, Alberto Lopez, and Amadeo Martinez (Bottom row L-R) Ursulita Lopez, Sarah Lopez and Virginia Martinez, dog "Lassie." Picture taken by Bonney in 1947.

School Years

When I was ten years old we moved to Alamosa, Colorado. Since I was a slightly built youngster, I did not participate in football or basketball, but I did take part in many other extracurricular activities. However, I preferred to spend time with my younger brother, Eddie. To this day, Eddie remains my best friend and confidante. With pride, I relate that Eddie is the owner of a very successful Alamosa insurance agency. He is also an antique business owner and real estate investor. He was the first Hispanic man to ever be appointed to the University of Northern Colorado Board of Trustees.

Anyone interested in becoming a governor or United States senator knows that in *el valle,* the road to success lies at Eddie Lopez' door. When Eddie Lopez invites you to spend the night at his home, it is virtually assured that the next morning, talk at the local coffee shops will give deference to your name. Though Eddie never graduated from high school, he has earned a PhD from the school of life.

One of Eddie's classmates was a boy named Leroy Edward Romero-a man that would ultimately be appointed to an office of prestige and honor. Imagine my delight when, as a grown man, I visited Spain and my host was our United States ambassador, the Honorable Edward L. Romero!

Yes! The boy who had been isolated from the rest of the world in *el valle*-a kid who used to wear patched overalls and grubby shoes, who ate tortillas with lard, was now our country's official representative to España.

Leroy was appointed to this office because of his financial success in New Mexico, his intelligence and affinity towards Spain. To those of us who grew up being called Spanish-Americans, it was proof positive that our roots were not shallow, that there was a connection linking the past to the present. A rarity in this country.

We are proudly, sometimes defiantly, American and still

Bonney and United States Ambassador to Spain, the Honorable Edward L. Romero, at the United States Embassy, Madrid Spain, October 1999.

not ashamed to find a family genealogy that links us back to Toledo or Granada, Spain, to the old world. For some of us, accepting the fact that we may have some Native American blood coursing through our veins is a problem that we typically cannot face. We can bring ourselves to say: *"Nosotros Mexicanos."* But, when speaking in English, many will still call ourselves Spanish-American. Despite that, our assertion and self-recognition of our native American roots is satisfying.

For example, I hear more Hispanics now talking about their Ute great grandmother. Our dark, blonde, blue-eyed, red-headed, *puro negrito*, coyote, mulatto kids already look like what the rest of the world will be when it finally gets its act together.

I quit school when I was twelve years old and found work in a restaurant as a dishwasher. After working twelve hours a day, I became convinced that I should return to school. I returned to the world of segregated classes (A, B & C), where Latinos rarely were allowed to take advanced study courses (i.e., college preparatory courses).

Class segregation was not the only problem that concerned me. On one occasion four of us (Eddie, my cousin Eliu Lopez, Leroy Romero and myself) skipped school to spend the afternoon at the Hooper Hot Springs a few miles north of Alamosa. Upon arrival at the pool, we were asked by the owner to leave because, "Mexicans are not allowed to swim here." Today the pool has new ownership and, as I understand, conditions have changed. But none of us has returned to swim there.

The fact that I returned to school pleased my mother that she convinced my school principal to grant me an eighth grade diploma, even though eighth grade commencement had long since passed. I think my mother was afraid that I would quit again and she wanted me to reflect upon this honor.

By the time I arrived in high school I had grown in confidence as well as in stature. By age sixteen, I had the status of a senior. Most of my friends were younger. I competed with some success in track and other sports and I was a top student, fully expecting to become the first member of my family to attend college.

This is where I encountered my dilemma, however. How would I pay for my education? In the 1950s, organizations giving scholarships to Latino students were virtually non-existent. Service groups such as the Lions Club, Elks or Rotary Club denied membership to Latinos. Clearly, these clubs were not inclined to give a grant to a Latina or Latino after having just rejected their parent for membership.

In 1950, I was fortunate to live in a town that had a state-supported local college-Adams State College. Tuition was affordable and I lived at home and worked part-time so I could enroll at the college. I majored in Business-a major rarely chosen by a person of Hispanic descent. In those days, most Latino students were inclined to major in Spanish or education with the intention of becoming a teacher. However, when I was in high school, I'd received my highest marks in

English and Math.

Now I must say something important about *mi familia*. I have never been without family. As I struggled through challenges and obstacles in my life, I was always sustained by my extended family. They helped me survive. I burned the midnight oil as a student and more than once I was the last one to leave the library. Still, I was never alone. The spirits of both my parents maintained their constant presence throughout my life. Their faith sustained me. Like so many parents, they couldn't always give me what they wanted in terms of financial support. Instead, they gave me all their love, support and encouragement.

Bonney and high school classmate Joe Vigil, (class of 1948). After graduation Joe joined the military than on to college. He obtained a PhD and became a Professor at Adams State College. At Adams State he coached track and took his world known teams to compete throughtout the country as well as in Russia and Korea.

Bonney playing the part of a "Pachuco". Young under-priviliged Spanish Americans living in the Valley during World War II did not know doctors, lawyers and businessmen that they could look up to for guidence or as mentors. The teenage Spanish Americans' heros were the young men being drafted to fight a war in places they didn't know existed, and activists of the time, the Zoot Suitors, feared by some, or *"Pachucos"*. To be a "Pachuco" was to belong or stand for a cause even if you didn't know the cause.

The Teacher

I graduated from Alamosa High School in 1948 at age 16. Two and a half years later with two years of college and a teaching certificate, I thought I'd try teaching. It's what my mother wanted... and I wanted to please her. I was 19 years old and still had no idea what direction to take in life. In those days you could get a Colorado certificate to teach in a grade school, however, you were required to take summer classes to get your certificate renewed annually.

My folks bought an old trunk, packed all my belongings and drove with me to San Antonio to live with my paternal grand parents, Grandpa Luis and Grandma Sarah. Since my annual salary was only $1,800 (payable over nine months) I couldn't afford room and board. My grand parents were more than happy and proud to have their grandson, "the teacher," live with them. They wanted me to sleep in the same large bedroom with them because it had a large pot belly stove and the winters could get very cold in San Antonio. During the winter months the temperature would often drop to 30 degrees below zero. Once, I recall, it was 50 below and it froze everything including the antifreeze in the automobile radiators.

I opted to have my own unheated bedroom with an outside entrance so I could go into town (Antonito) after my grandparents went to sleep (around 8:30 p.m.). It was perfect during the fall and spring months, but during the cold months I nearly froze to death. The blankets were a foot high and I was still cold. I'd wake up in the morning to find my jeans frozen stiff as a board and had to run to the kitchen to thaw them out near the kitchen wood burning stove.

Grandma had been up since 5 a.m. By 5:30 she had built a fire and started breakfast... fried potatoes, eggs, galletas (biscuits), *jamón* (ham or bacon) and of course fresh milk. Sometimes pancakes, too.

By 6 a.m. all of us were seated around the large kitchen table ready to say our morning prayers. We never skipped prayers. In fact, daily rosary after the evening meal was a required routine, no matter what else you scheduled. The table was huge and in the old days could accommodate 12 to 14 people during harvest times. Now, it was just grandpa, grandma, Uncle Luis "Louie" and myself. By 6 o'clock my clothes had thawed out; I'd washed, shaved and was prepared to go to my teaching job. Grandpa and uncle Luis had also shaved and washed up for breakfast. We normally took our baths at night before bedtime, taking turns since we had to heat the water on the stove and bathe in a small metal tub. For privacy we'd bathe in the dimly lit kitchen after everyone else went to bed.

Uncle Luis Lopez (father's older brother) had lived in a "*dispensita*" near my grandparents for several years. He'd lost his wife and his two grown children were living in another state. Since he was retired he had plenty of time to help my grandparents.

After helping grandma clean up and wash the morning dishes, I walked about a quarter mile to school. Classes started at 9:00 a.m. so I'd try to get there by 8:30. By the time I arrived some of the children would be in the playground or visiting with the janitor or one of the other teachers. The janitor usually came in at 6 a.m. and built a fire in each of three wood

Bonney Lopez, Principal of San Antonio Elementary School, 1952-53.

Staff for the San Antone Panther Yearbook, 1952-53.

Ross Duran, Frank Lopez, Mary Lou Romero, Helen Gallegos, Eusebio Duran.

burning pot belly stoves... one in each class room.
By the time the children arrived the rooms were nice and warm. It was up to the teachers and / or the students to keep the fires burning in the stoves throughout the school day. Classes were broken into three groups. Kindergarten through second grades was in one room, third through fifth grades in another and sixth through eighth grades in the third room. The third room was partitioned off within the gymnasium.

The first year I taught 12 to 15 students consisting of third fourth and fifth graders. Students sat in rows of old fashioned school desks. A separate row for each grade. Sometimes there were more students in one row because there may be more third graders than fifth graders, for example. I worked with one class at a time by bringing them up to the front of the room where they would all sit on a home made wooden bench.

There we would work on reading, arithmetic geography or whatever the subject. By being in front, the students would not be distracted by students in the other classes. Those students remained in their desks. Working in front also gave us easy access to the blackboards. Students from other classes were not kept from participating in discussions taking place at the front bench as long as they added to the discussion, did not distract those sitting on the bench and as long as they got their own work completed on time.

Learning to read was perhaps the most important

Bonney in front of the old San Antonio elementary school,
December 2001.

San Antonio elementary school, January 1953.
Note Bonney's 1950 Ford Crestliner in front.

San Antonio elementary school as it looks today.

subject. Even though the children lived in the United States and most of their ancestors arrived in this country before the Pilgrims, through no fault of their own, they were isolated from an English-speaking environment. English was their second language and they were required to master it. In most of the homes only Spanish was spoken. Therefore, school children had to be constantly reminded to speak English in school so that the second language would become easier to learn.

To make things even more difficult, the school district didn't have sufficient funds to provide books. Textbooks could not be taken home and could only be used in the classroom. All books were kept in a locked room, distributed in the morning and returned to the locked room at the end of the school day. Only workbooks and weekly papers purchased by the students could be taken home. Most of the families in the community at the time did not subscribe to a weekly newspaper, let alone a daily paper. Some families could not afford a radio. Television was unheard of.

I had been working for a daily newspaper while in college and knew that they always had a surplus of unsold papers left over at the end of each day. I spoke to the publisher/editor and explained my predicament. He agreed to give me as many unsold copies of the daily newspaper as I wanted. Every weekend I'd visit his office in Alamosa and pick out those issues containing articles, pictures etc. I thought would interest my students.

First thing Monday morning we'd begin by talking

about what we did over the weekend. This would lead to things that happened in other places. I'd mention a little about something I read just enough to get their interest. Then I'd tell them we didn't have time to get into the details but I was going to leave several issues of last week's newspaper on the table. "If you need help in finding an article let me know," I'd say. Before long I'd see a group of girls reading "juicy" articles and giggling. The boys always read the comic strips. Later, I started bringing old issues of the Denver Post and Rocky Mountain News. My kids were allowed to take the newspapers home and keep them after the paper had been in the classroom one week.

It wasn't all work and study. There were plenty of little incidents, as I recall, that had nothing to do with studies. For example, the boys were always volunteering to go out to the well and fetch a fresh bucket of drinking water. The water would get warm in the room and they wanted cold water. The problem was it would take two boys an unusually long time to return with the water. Sometimes the water was warm by the time they got back and the well was only a short distance from the building. Another distraction was the students not waiting until recess time to use the restrooms. By raising one or two fingers, they would signal the teacher that they needed to go to the outhouse. Sometimes more than one wanted to go out at the same time. This meant they had other plans... maybe to sneak a handmade cigarette.

One time a young boy brought a handful of twenty-two shells (live bullets) and threw them in the potbelly stove. When the shells started popping everyone seemed to know what was happening except the teacher. Fortunately the stove was made of heavy metal and the bullets only made dents all over the inside of the pot belly stove. Never found out who did it… but I had a good idea. In spite of all this, my kids turned out pretty good. I see some of them when I visit the valley or I run into them in Denver and other places. They have good jobs and fine families…. even grandchildren.

The second year I taught sixth through eight grades and served as principal and coach. My annual salary had increased to $2,000 (still payable in nine months). Now I was married and living in the dispensita with my new wife, Lucille. The teaching routine was similar except the students were older and their needs were different. English was not a problem with this group, but there was a lack of interest in reading. Because this was a farming community, attendance for a few of the older students was not perfect. Some were needed to help their parents in the spring and fall. A few had been held back and were pretty close to the same age as the teacher, but they were all good and honest kids. I just needed to come up with some good ideas to keep them interested in school.

Once I got to know them better and met their parents, we began working on different projects to make school attendance more fun. We started to get some of the parents involved through the parent-teacher association. The classroom set up was similar, the desks were old, the wooden bench up in front and etc.

We added public speaking, plays, sports, dances and other activities always working at enhancing the student's reading proficiency. Some of the students had natural musical talents and we encouraged them to use them in school programs. Students provided the music for school dances. They seemed to be natural born singers with beautiful voices. They produced a Christmas play, translated it into Spanish and presented it to the whole community.

At the beginning of the year they decided to publish a yearbook. They organized the staff, assigned the various tasks, including photographers, and by the end of the school year had published the first and only yearbook for the school. The fifty-year-old "San Antone Panther" is now a treasured book, containing pictures, names and events of a school that no longer exists.

The students also formed a club to raise funds by charging the public to attend some of their activities. They used the funds to acquire a PA system and a movie projector

During WPA days, the Federal government had helped fund a gymnasium for the small school. The gym could be split off into two large classrooms; one was used for the upper grades, the other contained a stage for plays etc. Because this gym was still in good condition we started a boys basketball team. A winning team was made up of fifth, sixth, seventh and eighth graders. Size didn't matter as long as they could play. The girls made up the pep club, cheerleaders and etc. The gym was not regulation size and the baskets were lower so shorter boys, with plenty of practice, were great players. Since we were one of the few grade schools with a gym, we invited other teams to play against us. Our team was more experienced and usually won most of the tournaments.

Lucille, too, was very active in helping with the programs. She even substituted for me when I was ill for a day or two. In fact, the students preferred her as a teacher. I wonder why?

The time I spent teaching in San Antonio is perhaps one of the most memorable periods in my life. Some may think this had to have been a boring experience, but the things I learned about myself could not have been learned in the best of colleges. I later lived a similar experience in Honduras.

MI FAMILIA

Lucille

While in college, at age nineteen, by fortunate chance I found the love of my life. The price I paid to enter the dance hall in nearby La Jara where my life would be changed forever was only fifty cents. This parent-supervised dance lasted five hours, from 5:00 p.m. to 10:00 p.m. and no alcohol was ever allowed on the premises.

Lucille Marquez was not yet seventeen years old. From the moment I saw this slim, graceful girl gazing knowingly and confidently at me across a crowded floor with wide, intelligent, dark brown eyes, my chest got tight. I could hardly breathe. I just knew that I wanted her forever. Although I was older, I didn't feel a bit in control of the

My in-laws, Lucille's parents, Daniel and Beatrice (Muniz) Marquez on their wedding day in Capulin, Colorado, February 3, 1913.

situation. I knew that I had to convince her of my worthiness; and that she would not be conquered or dominated easily. I had to earn her attention, and it took two months before she favored me with a kiss. She was a popular high school girl, a homecoming queen and a highly sought after prize by every young man in the region.

I think that the only reason her parents gave me permission to court her was because I enjoyed dressing up in a suit and presented myself in a respectable manner. To be certain, I quickly forgot the other girl I had been dating.

Lucille and I frequently conspired to see each other as much as we could, even going to the point of once having an accommodating non-romantic male friend escort her to a no-outsiders-allowed school dance. This friend was a handsome, athletic football hero and considered quite the catch in the community. How Lucille talked Ignes Lucero (who later became a well known surgeon in Denver) into being a friendly foil (rather than presenting himself as a candidate for consideration himself), remains a mystery to me to this day. They passed the scrutiny of the guards at the door and I managed to sneak in through a side door and enjoyed a few spins around the floor with my sweetheart that evening.

Our courtship lasted a year before we were married. Our wedding celebration lasted three days and was complete with violins and the traditional wedding march through town. The march was led by both of my grandfathers, with everyone joining in behind. Lucille's brother Joe and sister-in-law Faye were the *padrinos* (best man and matron of honor). The simple wedding band that I placed on her finger cost $35.00. In truth, though, ours was a lifelong courtship. She was my first thought in the morning. I adored her and still do. My grief for her loss is unabated, even after sixteen years without her.

Bonney and Lucille on their wedding, June 18, 1951 in Antonito, Colorad. Flower girl is Lucille's niece, Philomena "Mena" (Gonzales) Gallegos.

When we returned from our honeymoon, I must have thought that Lucille and I were going to live on love because I didn't have a job. Eddie, my brother, was working at a filling station and he convinced me to work part time with him. Eddie and I always had a deal or racket going to make an extra buck or two, it seemed. During the middle of the week, I'd deliver the Alamosa Courier Newspaper to the surrounding towns of Monte Vista, Del Norte and Center. I then started teaching in San Antonio, the same tiny school district where my own education begun. Lucille and I lived in a two-room *dispensa* (shed), next to Grandpa Luis and Grandma Sarah who lived nearby. Our

ⓘ PUBLIC RESOURCES

Post Office	2080 S Holly St 1-303-639-9867
Governor Information	Gov. Bill Ritter (D) 1-303-866-2471 www.nga.org/governors
US Senate	Senators Sen. Wayne Allard (R) Sen. Ken Salazar (D) 1-202-224-3121
US House	Find your state representative 1-202-224-3121 www.house.gov
Government Resources	FirstGov U.S. portal for government info www.firstgov.gov 1-800-FED-INFO
Voter ᵗⁱⁱⁱᵗⁱᵒⁿ	Election Assistance Commission Find forms and information at

★★★★ HOUSEHOLD SERVICES

Automobile Insurance	GEICO- 15 minutes could save you 15% or more. Call 1-800-554-0286 or go to geico.com.
Satellite TV	DIRECTV Satellite TV 1-888-710-7849 $200 Cash Back Offer!
Installation Services	The Home Depot Expert Installation Services Call 888-332-6761, or visit www.homedepot.com/install
Phone Services	Qwest 1-866-375-6683 (MOVE) Get the phone services you need at the price you want.
Newspaper	Save when you subscribe to The Denver Post or Rocky Mountain News! Call 1-303-832-3232
Medicare Health Care	SecureHorizons from UnitedHealthcare

OLD ADDRESS:

ISIDORA SHIRKEY
6801 E MISSISSIPPI AVE APT C302
DENVER CO 80224-3612

NEW ADDRESS:

0009338-64573199

*************AUTO**3-DIGIT 802

ISIDORA SHIRKEY
895 S MONACO PKWY RM 14B # RM
DENVER CO 80224-1501

home for almost a year consisted of, a bedroom and kitchen, with an outhouse close by. My Grandparents gladly provided me with this free *casita*, across from their own living quarters.

Our sources of entertainment included finding a buck or two for an occasional movie, visiting with family and talking or playing card games with tío Alfonso (my dad's brother) and his wife, Tía Pauline.

We eventually moved back to Alamosa so I could finish college and major in business. College housing was old Army barracks. Lucille worked at the Alamosa Abstract office and I worked part-time at a local drug store. During my last quarter in college, the superintendent of the Florence School District happened to be teaching summer classes at the college. He told me about an opening in the Business department at Florence High School. Lucille and I discussed it and determined that this might just be the door being opened for us. My application to the FBI had not been accepted by J. Edgar Hoover. Also, the move might provide better opportunities for my children. We felt that, if anything, the potential for a better education was there. We had to at

Bonney and Lucille's first home in 1951, close to Grandpa Luis and Grandma Sarah's home in San Antonio, Colorado. This picture was taken in the 1980s.

least try. I applied and was hired immediately for a salary of $3,300 a year (August 1953). We certainly needed the money because my son, Micheal, was born in 1952 in Alamosa.

Less than twenty months later, he was diagnosed with juvenile diabetes. Within the next few years, our other three children (Jim, Ronnie and Jilda) were born in Florence.

In Florence, we lived in a studio apartment with a combination living-room/bedroom. It was so small that when we pulled down our Murphy bed, it was impossible to open the front door. That was where Lucille and I made all our important life decisions.

Even after we had a little more money, what mattered the most in the world were private moments that we shared, alone. Lucille and I quietly continued talking about the consequential and inconsequential matters of our lives. We decided how we were going to shape ourselves, raise our children and what was of value and importance in our lives. Fundamentally, any decisions of importance or having to do with character remained unshakable and unaltered in our minds.

In later years, when Lucille and I went into the business of buying and selling real estate, this was our constant habit. It propelled us on towards greater success in business as well as private matters. Our end of the day kitchen table talk continued throughout the years-from the time our little ones had been put to bed until well after they were grown and had left home. This was a habit that we never wanted to abandon.

Changing Professions

For the next three years, my summer vacations from Florence High School were spent working at the CF&I (Colorado Fuel and Iron) steel mill to earn extra income. This was a welcome respite. Lucille clearly enjoyed being away from the isolated, confining lifestyle that we had to endure in Florence. However, it was there that I received a hefty dose of reality.

I had expected to be offered some sort of office job at the company. It turned out that my employers viewed me as just another *Mejicano*. I had thought, given my education, that I would be offered a cushy office job. Instead, they

Florence High School in Florence, Colorado. This picture was taken in 1954. The outside of the building has not changed; however, the inside was almost completely remodled and is not as attractive as it was back then.

handed me a pair of goggles and gloves and sent me to the wire mill. While I was there, I witnessed three fatal industrial accidents. This became a turning point in my life, and more than ever, convinced me that my fate was not going to be an ordinary one. I was unwavering and determined to make a distinctive mark in life.

As a teacher in Florence, I enjoyed the respect of the community and increase in salary to $3600.00 a year. For the early 1950s, this was considered an excellent salary. My reputation in town was one of good standing, and I was equally held in high regard amongst my peers and students. This all changed when I made the decision to help establish a union for the local chapter of the Colorado Federation of Teachers (a sub-union of AFL-CIO).

Florence was not an entirely progressive town. It was a community that got left behind, simply because the major highway bypassed the town by several miles. Most of the

coal mines were closing, leaving few opportunities for employment there. It was a town that had a hard time keeping up. At times, was resistant to proposals

Bonney Lopez, Florence High School Business Teacher, 1953-56.

and changes that might alter its course.

In those days, school power was not democratically distributed among staff members. Hispanics were considered subservient to the predominantly Caucasian population there, and, from my perspective, treated almost as indentured servants to the presiding majority. Barto Babitz, the new superintendent of schools, was autocratic/dictatorial and unwelcoming of any changes or initiatives that might bring his authority into question.

"You'd better stop this kind of organizing or there will be trouble to bear," he warned. Yet, I was foolish and proud. I ignored his not-so-veiled threats and continued with my unionist activities. Mr. Babitz fired me. Actually, if he could have tarred and feathered me, he would have done so. My contract for the following year was never renewed. Along with the termination letter came his own private message: "As long as you live in this town, you will be a thorn in my side, Bonney," he said.

Quickly the word got around that I was "not part of the team." I began to notice other teachers avoiding me, not wanting to be seen talking to me. It was bad enough that I was being ostracized, but the teachers' wives, too, were avoiding Lucille. She was not invited to their social functions any more and they would cross the street to keep from meeting her face to face.

As Lucille and I grew together in our marriage, I knew that no matter what the crisis, I could depend on her to be there for me. She was about to be put to the test… a big "stand by your man" challenge. Lucille's response was typical: "We'll do fine, Bonney. Do what you want to do."

With a wife and family to support, I was now out of work, but not out of ideas. My approach to teaching had always been based on practical application rather than on the theoretical. My business students learned accounting principals by actually keeping the books of small area businesses. During the summer break, when classes were not in session, I carried on with these assignments. Through these classes, I developed a client base.

My first client was John "Colonel" Fabrizio, co-owner of the local Coors distributorship (Fabrizio Brothers). Upon hearing that I was unemployed, he immediately offered me a contract to handle his bookkeeping needs full time. Charlie Salardino, owner of New Music Company, was my second client. Other merchants soon followed the Colonel's influential endorsement and, thus, I was in business for myself.

It seemed like the Italian business community came to my rescue. Perhaps because they, too, had struggled to start their own businesses in a not so friendly environment. Bankers, normally a good source of referrals for accountants, occasionally assured me that they would send tax clients in my direction, but nothing ever materialized. Thanks to the Fabrizios, the Salardinos, the Bertas and the Camerlos, my business began to prosper.

The same bankers, in jest, more than once encouraged me to search out government assistance such as Federal 8-A contracts and affirmative action programs available to minorities. I was determined to compete for business just like everyone else and never considered such "encouragement."

I wanted to be more than a bookkeeper, however. Academic course work at Adams State College had provided me with a solid foundation in business orientation. But the small school was still not suited to offer its students' certification in advanced studies. I wanted to become a Certified Public Accountant. On weekends and nights I'd take graduate CPA correspondence courses from La Salle University in Chicago. I embarked on a self-imposed, demanding regime of home study and weekend seminars. Lucille gave me tremendous support keeping the kids quiet so that I could study. They still remember all of the "quiet times" we had.

I also added daily mass to my regime and Lucille and I prayed constantly together. Our faith grew and we realized, that to achieve what we wanted we also needed to provide additional time to God.

There were about eighteen other accountants from Pueblo, and the surrounding area, with a like ambition who took the statewide CPA exams at the same time. They all had more education. Most had attended better schools, had better instruction and they had the advantage of financial support. None of us passed the CPA exam the first time around. For me, though, failure has never been an option.

The Florence School superintendent who fired me

caused indisputable injury and financial hardship to my family. When he fired me, he also caused me to examine my goals and ambitions in life. Frankly, he did me a favor. Perhaps I would have gone on to accomplish many of the same things that I did in my life anyway, perhaps not. What ultimately could have brought me down ended uplifting me.

Years later, the same man who fired me became my good friend. When I established my business, I went to him and made my peace. When he was dying of cancer, I was at his bedside.

You destroy your enemy when you make them your friend (Romans 12:20).

Long-term anger and grudge-bearing is simply not an option in my life.

In my view, when you close your heart off to forgiveness, you close yourself off from being forgiven. When the famed South-African leader, Nelson Mandela, forgave his oppressors that imprisoned him for thirty years, he truly liberated himself.

The Loss of Lucille

In 1962 my bookkeeping practice was doing well I had just passed my CPA exams and became the only CPA in Fremont County. We were long overdue for a family vacation. Lucille and I decided to go to the World's Fair in New York City and then on to Washington, D.C. for more sight-seeing. We had never been east of Pueblo, Colorado and we wanted to broaden our horizons.

Side trips were going to happen by impulse, rather than by necessity. One such trip was a ride to Boston. We packed up our new station wagon and away we went! Boston is such a wonderful part of our nation's history but our main reason for visiting was to experience the Boston Institute of Music. Ms. Eleanor McCandless, a neighbor and our children's piano teacher in Florence, Colorado, had studied there.

As always, Lucille made all the travel arrangements. Ours would be a three-week trip, she decided. After years of sacrifice and barely getting by, we had paid our dues and we were looking forward to the experience of visiting other parts of our country. What made this trip even more special was the fact that my life partner was to share in this pleasure. Lucille so richly deserved this indulgence and I was finally in a position to give it to her.

We fell in love with Washington, D.C. Our Congressman, J. Edgar Chenoweth took time from his busy legislative schedule and personally escorted us everywhere, from the Lincoln Memorial to the Smithsonian Institute. Chenoweth, a member of Congress, was acting as our tour guide! New York City and the World's Fair were fabulous, too. There we saw our first Broadway play, visited Central Park, the Statue of Liberty, Radio City Music Hall and the Empire State Building.

We also had another treat: Jack Dempsey. The former world heavyweight champion entertained our boys at his

The Lopez family visiting the nation's Capitol with their congressman as their guide. Micheal, Bonney, Lucille, Congressman Chenoweth and Jimmy.

restaurant, after learning that we hearkened from a town near his birthplace, Manassa, Colorado. The "Manassa Mauler", as Jack was called, turned out to be a supreme gentleman. When I showed up at his restaurant without the required jacket, he was quick to say: "I'm the boss, don't worry about it." The kids were thrilled when he gifted them with a variety of souvenirs.

During our trip, we ate things that we'd only seen in magazines and movies-crab, lobster, etc. It was from one of these meals that Lucille got quite sick. Early on, doctors felt that maybe the shellfish caused her liver disease but we later found out this was not the case. Little did we know that this seemingly minor medical incident was a forewarning of increasingly worse things to come. For the remaining twenty-four years of her life, Lucille never enjoyed perfect health again. Later, she would endure several surgeries and suffer from advanced liver disease.

Lucille was an extraordinary person. Kindness exuded from her. Typically, a poor family would respond to a knock on their door, only to find Lucille standing there with an armload of food and clothing. She understood how difficult it was for unemployed miners and their families and others like them, who had no financial means for sustenance. It was not an unusual condition for families at that time to be struggling to put food on their table. Later, when we moved to our new home in Canon City, Lucille continued to minister to many local people. She never rushed home at the stroke of 5:00 p.m. When most people ended their business day, she was still out there helping. The door to our home was open twenty-four hours a day to anyone who might come to visit or participate in a prayer meeting.

It was now the mid 1980s and time for another family conference. By this time, I'd sold our business and was caring for Lucille on a full-time basis. During that time John and Dora Gonzales (Lucille's sister and brother-in-law) came to live with us for a few months. Dora was a tremendous comfort to both of us. When Lucille could barely keep down food, Dora would prepare *atole* and *poliadas* (sugar, flour and cinnamon). These New-Mexican comfort foods kept her alive physically, emotionally and spiritually.

As time wore on, my wife became increasingly sick. Vacations to Spain and Mexico were replaced by more and more trips to Colorado General Hospital in Denver. Dr. Meda, at Colorado General Hospital, had diagnosed Lucille with primary biliary cirrhosis years ago. He had treated her as her illness worsened over the years.

By this time our children were grown and living away from home. Jilda and Ronnie were in college, Jim was in medical school and Mike was in Washington D.C.

When her condition was no longer tolerable, Dr. Meda told us: "The only way Lucille will survive is with a liver transplant." We all met at Jimmy's home to discuss it further as a family. Another of Jimmy's medical school professors (who, by this time, was practicing in Pittsburgh) had performed the first transplant at Colorado General Hospital. He was considered the top transplant doctor in the country.

Jimmy consulted him regarding his mother's current health status and became convinced that she must be taken to the Mayo Clinic.

We arrived at the Rochester, Minnesota Mayo Clinic on July 1, 1986 and stayed there the rest of the month. Our daily routine consisted of: up at 6 am, light breakfast at 7 am, help Lucille to her wheelchair, go from clinic to clinic until 6 p.m. A light dinner and back to the hotel room located within the Mayo complex ended the day.

Everything appeared to be going along just fine until it came to admit Lucille to the hospital in preparation for the liver transplant. Then it seemed the whole world came tumbling down on me. The very fine print of our insurance policy excluded transplants (something we were not aware of). I suddenly learned we were left without medical coverage. Both Medicare and our insurance company refused to pay her medical expenses! Though the Mayo Clinic is the cream of the crop in diagnostics and medical care, it is not free of charge. We were told that the transplant would cost $200,000 and, if not covered by insurance, had to be paid up front.

"I'll pay this personally... I'll be back tomorrow... I'll get the money for you", I told them. Lucille never learned of my predicament. She just sat quietly in her wheel chair awaiting my decision. I told her we would have to come back the next day and immediately phoned my bank in Canon City. "Send me a bank draft to cover Lucille's medical expenses. I want it now, not tomorrow," I insisted. Within minutes, Bill Paolino at the First National Bank in Canon City, authorized letters of credit and sent the hospital a telegram. Lucille was admitted to the Mayo Clinic Hospital first thing next morning. Pre-surgical examinations and diagnostics began. We then met with a medical team who would perform the operation when a compatible donor was found.

Then came yet another bombshell. We were told that Lucille's operation was "too risky" and they were afraid it couldn't be done. Lucille responded with a fierce lecture: "You're afraid of failure and you're protecting yourselves. You don't want to blow your 'success' statistics. I'm not afraid, why should you be?"

The Mayo Clinic then handed us a bill for $91,000, despite their refusal to perform Lucille's transplant operation. Ultimately, a kind social worker arranged to have our debt completely erased from our tab. After Lucille died, I received a statement from the Mayo Clinic marked "Paid In Full."

The Mayo staff offered us another alternative-a hospital in Omaha, Nebraska. We looked to the counsel and experience of our son, Jimmy (who himself had already undergone a kidney transplant in Minneapolis on August 15, 1984). Jimmy's colleagues endorsed Lucille's referral to this hospital and all was set for the surgical procedure.

By the first of August, Lucille had returned home from the Mayo Clinic and her health had deteriorated significantly. She was more ill and frail than she had ever been. On Sunday morning, I called our family physician and dear friend, Dr. John Buglewicz, who counseled me to put Lucille on oxygen support and transport her to Colorado General Hospital.

The entire family flocked to Lucille's bedside that Sunday morning. Her older brother, Joe Marquez, wept inconsolable tears. Then there was Jimmy. He was cut from the same mold as many young doctors. He was a consummate professional, but he also had a stubborn tendency to dress in a scruffy manner. This habit, he'd always known, was an irritating point of contention with his mother. On the day that Lucille was waiting, at Colorado General Hospital, for the ambulance to come and take her to the airport and then on to Omaha, Jimmy walked into his mother's hospital room with a grin on his face. He was dressed sharp as a tack, with polished shoes and a classy tie. He was the epitome of the successful young doctor with whom his mama was so proud. Though her smile was weak and her face was ashen, she managed to murmur, "Finally…"

The ride to the airport was desperate. We ran out of oxygen en-route. Lucille was deathly sick and hungry and she longed for the homemade tortillas her friend made for her the Sunday we left home. We wept and prayed on the plane to Omaha and to the University of Nebraska Medical Center. When we arrived, an apartment adjacent to the hospital had been prepared for our stay. It was complete with oxygen and other medical equipment.

The medical team in Omaha was positive and encouraging. "Yes, we will succeed." The surgery was planned to take place in early August, but we still needed to find a donor. Another barrage of diagnostic tests and examinations ensued. Lucille's health continued to decline. I spent most of my time in her hospital room, away from the apartment. I wanted to be no more than a footstep away from her.

We talked and then talked some more. As always, we were frank with one another, without pretense. We'd shared three decades of open, honest and loving communication. Though painful, this was a great consolation to both of us as we lovingly prepared one another for the inevitable. As always, we talked about our hopes, dreams and expectations. Now we talked about her imminent departure from earth. We talked about her estate matters and forthcoming funeral services. Lucille held my hand and consoled me. She calmly told me how her possessions should be distributed.

One morning Lucille had a peaceful demeanor. She was elated and began singing in praise. There was a true angelic glow about her. She wanted to phone her family and did so. One after another she talked about how great she felt and that everything was going to be OK. Then suddenly she began choking and spitting up blood. Doctors rushed to her side and told me she had to go in for emergency surgery. She was hemorrhaging from her esophagus.

In Denver, our children were already rushing to make their way to Omaha. "Hurry! Hurry!" I implored of them. "Please hurry!" The surgery lasted over ten hours. Lucille had received twenty-four pints of blood. When my children arrived she was still in surgery, but now we were together as a family. The doctors came out to talk to us... it wasn't good. Lucille continued to bleed but they did the best they could to stop it. The next twenty-four hours would be the most critical. Doctors asked to talk to us the first thing the following morning.

We knew what we were going to be asked. Before we met with them, we made our way to a nearby chapel and prayed.

The doctors were not hopeful... it was now our decision. Should we agree to allow the medical staff to disconnect the life support system? Jimmy spoke. "Dad, we have to let her go..." We agreed this was the merciful thing to do and without argument, informed them of our decision.

Lucille made her own decision. Without being taken off the support... at 4:00 p.m. that day, Lucille died.

I stayed at her bedside... alone... together, for the last time.

A deep-pitted wave of anguish coursed through my body. My hands shook and my body heaved in deep gasping breaths. It was as if I, too, was fighting to live... to breathe. I emitted a painful moan from my throat. I had no desire to live or leave my beloved wife.

We spent our last time as a family together with Lucille. We began sharing stories about all of the good times and as a release we found humor - our consolation.

We flew back to Denver, in the same plane with Lucille's body, then drove on home to Canon City. *Como siempre*, we traveled as *familia*. With Lucille had come family and friends who had been attracted to her inner beauty. Now, I was alone. I was no longer an extension of Lucille. Nor was I able to bask in her incredible light. Yet, I know that I have friends, old and new, who truly care for me. My sons and daughter have never abandoned me. My grandchildren are quite fond of me, I know. I have the respect of colleagues. I have also had other relationships. Yet, I feel severed-incomplete… without beloved Lucille beside me.

I often reflect that one does not necessarily choose the love of your life or your ultimate mate. There are forces

Lucille's "Daily Prayer of Commitment" inscribed on the family headstone at Lakeside Cemetery in Canon City, Colorado. Lucille's, Micheal's and Jimmy's ashes are buried here.

greater than ourselves. One can either choose to run from love or to stay the distance and allow love to happen. Staying the distance is what reaps abundance, I've learned. Lucille was my love and my mate. From the first moment I saw her, I ran towards her… and love.

I have a strong and unshakable faith in God and every Sunday, when I go to church and take communion, I feel as if I'm visiting with my beloved wife, Lucille and my sons, Micheal and Jimmy. Their presence to me in church or at their gravesite in Canon City's Lakeside cemetery is more emotional than spiritual. I truly feel as if we are only separated for just a brief moment.

Before Lucille died, she became devoted to the newly emerging aspects of a post-Vatican II theology. Her conscious and deliberate faith was unquestioning; borne from a long history of devoted and faithful family members and community influence. No longer was her faith one that she had to practice simply because our ancestors carried a cross with them as they settled in the new southwest four centuries ago. The simplistic philosophy of "pray, pay and obey" was no longer acceptable, even to Hispanics, who sought more from their spiritual faith.

Lucille desired a mature understanding and relationship within Catholicism. Her objective led her far to Saint Mary's University, in San Antonio Texas, to study Catholicism for three months, beyond the confines of our small southern Colorado community.

By today's standards, Lucille might be considered an

ordinary, subjugated, stay-at-home mother, as she did little work outside the home after our children were born. Never, though, was she anything other than my complete partner. No topic was off-limits for us. For example, our daily pattern included animated discussions of how I might respond to a particular business problem that arose at the office. Lucille was not only strong of opinion but she was also insightful and discerning; able to perceive subtle nuances in most situations and in most people. I relied on her insights and perceptions, as these were things that might often escape me. I recall many nights in our humble first home where we had many talks.

My friend and lover, Lucille, stayed close by me; yet she never stood still. She also refused to let me stand still-to be less of a man or to be anything less than what was my potential. She accepted my desire to be different-my desire to take risks and not settle for the ordinary, in job, career or life.

It must have taken more than a bit of courage to explain to curious, well-meaning relatives why I (a college graduate), was unwilling to settle for a high-status, low paying position of a teacher. The height of honor in the Latino community was to have a job where you wore a *corbata* (a necktie). No matter what the pay, if you wore out the seat of your pants before you wore out the knees, you were somebody to be admired and respected.

Lucille simply trusted me. She didn't see a skinny, cocky boy, but a man with capacities, talents and gifts, just waiting to be revealed. I had the formal education and Lucille had the wisdom. She never demanded the impossible from me. She simply expected that I would make proper use of myself. Anything less would not have been acceptable. She expected me to do the possible and to confront difficult situations or problems as opportunities.

Lucille was more than just a housewife. She found time to work after our children were grown and away from home. Her repertoire of employment included positions in jewelry sales, manager of an abstract office and as an accountant. She also had a talent most did not know. She was an artist. We continue to treasure her beautiful paintings to this day.

Besides working part-time, Lucille found time to meet and become friends with female neighbors who enticed her into joining a bridge club and playing tennis. She was an adept and proficient learner and soon became a tournament caliber bridge player.

Lucille was my wife, friend, partner, lover, confidante and companion. What more can I say? She was my equal in every respect and capable in more than a few matters. I never stood taller than when I knelt to rub her feet, hold her hand or caress her brow, when she was tired or weeping without shame... when she was weak and dying. The more she suffered, the faster she aged. Yet, the more beautiful she appeared to me. And I loved her all the more.

My Sons Micheal and Jimmy

We expect to bury our parents before we ever bury a child. In marriage, one mate usually leaves this life before the other. What we don't expect is our child to die before us.

When I was a young man, I knew many Latino parents who had buried their sons who were killed in the Second World War and in Korea. Thousands of Latino mothers saved their folded American flags in wooden chests that could fill

 a dozen stadiums. Men and women my age buried sons who were killed in Vietnam. One can never expect to have

Jimmy, age 9 months and Micheal, age 3 at home, 4th and Pikes in Florence, June 1954. Jim was born in Florence and Mike was born in Alamosa.

illness or disease strike down a son or a daughter, in the prime of their life, when everything that is good seems to be just in front of them.

Diabetes is an insidious disease that typically runs in families and is prevalent among Hispanics. Diabetes is to the Latino community what Sickle Cell Anemia is to African Americans. Many of us are genetically predisposed to this devastating medical condition. There are two types of diabetes: Type II occurs in adults and in conjunction with poor eating habits. Type I (juvenile diabetes), is like a bug, and occurs typically in children. Juvenile diabetes destroys the pancreas and the sufferer, almost always, must take insulin. Both my sons had inherited this cruelly devastating disease-a disease much more severe than Type II diabetes. My anguish is compounded by the knowledge that my sons did not enjoy a childhood free of medical maladies.

James Joseph Lopez, M.D. receiving his Doctorate Degree at CU Medical School graduation ceremonies in Denver May 1980.

My son, Micheal was only eighteen months old when he contracted childhood diabetes. Jimmy was eleven years old when he was first diagnosed. Both of them were careful to eat properly, exercise regularly, and take insulin to combat this disease. Throughout their teenage years and into their twenties, they enjoyed relatively good health. Jimmy even succeeded in pursuing a medical degree. The one positive thing this disease gave my sons was a drive to succeed and to "live life".

Painfully, they still died too early. Jimmy, our second son, was the first to die at age 33 in 1989. By 1984, Jimmy was in kidney failure and was forced to endure painful tri-weekly dialysis treatments. His medical practice in Limon, where he was fulfilling a school loan obligation, was interrupted. He was in need of a kidney transplant and

appropriately enough, his best friend, sister Jilda, turned out to be the most compatible donor available. On

Bonney, Mike and Jim, weekly golf games at South Suburban Country Club in Littleton, Colorado, 1988.

August 15, 1984, in Minneapolis, Jimmy received a kidney from his sister, Jilda. Five years later, however, the insidious disease attacked again. Jimmy had endured pain for several years longer than he should have because he knew that if he went into the hospital he would probably die. He was immunosuppressed because of the transplant. In a hospital, infection is a high risk. One of Jimmy's legs was amputated. Ever the optimist and fighter, Jimmy planned this event with care. "As long as they amputate below the knee I can continue my work," he said.

Doctors were forced to remove his leg above the knee. Heartbreak.

The young man who prepared himself so well for the medical profession was now told that he couldn't pursue his lifelong dream. All the study of biology and chemistry, graduating from fine schools (University of Denver and CU Medical School), now seemed wasted.

Jimmy was wracked with pain and he knew his inexorable fate. He went into the hospital in November and never got out. There was one complication after another and on January 3 1989, Jimmy died.

Jimmy was a pistol as a kid, though he was a straight "A" student at Holy Cross Abbey high school in Canon City (a private school), where we'd moved when my emerging accounting business had far outgrown Florence's city limits. Holy Cross Abbey (for young men) and St. Scholastica Academy (for young women) were considered two of the finest private schools in the West. Holy Cross students came from far-reaching ends of the country.

Lucille and I were very fortunate to have such exceptional academic institutions located literally in our back yard. We also wanted our children to be challenged academically. I look back with fondness at my own public school experiences and feel as though they honed and toughened me. Still, I know that the education I received in tiny San Antonio and Alamosa would not have prepared me adequately for the rigors of a top-notch college.

Micheal Lopez in Washington D.C. working as Legislative Aide for Congressman Ray Kogovsek, 1978-84.

Joelle and Gabriel Lopez, Micheal's children, Colorado Governors Mansion in Denver. Gabriel was presented his second annual Scholarship award from British Petroleum, 2001.

Micheal graduated in 1970; Jimmy graduated in 1972 and Ron graduated in 1975–all from the Abbey. Jilda, our only daughter, was a 1978 graduate of St. Scholastica Academy.

Though Micheal was a bright student, when he attended the University of Denver on a full scholarship, he wasn't ready for the opportunity and was not able to move beyond his freshman year. Though we were disappointed in Mike, Lucille and I didn't berate him. We always expected our children to rise or fail on their own. Additionally, we believed that it was not our job to carry our children all the way; that it was simply our job to get them to the starting line. Because of this, we opted to allow our children the opportunity to pay for their college education on their own. Micheal admitted that he really blew his chance in this area. As the saying goes: "After enlightenment, comes the laundry." He realized what he had done and now he was ready to face the consequences. Rather than hide out in disgrace, Mike came home to face the music and answer all the embarrassing questions about how his life at DU was going.

I must mention that Micheal was a very talented musician. He had a natural musical talent from the time he was very small. He played the piano at home and the trumpet in the school band. After a days work, you would often find him playing his electronic piano, using his earphones, composing music.

When Micheal was in high school I once asked him what he wanted to study in college. He said that he wanted to study music and become a music teacher. Having been disappointed in the teaching profession myself, I responded, "What in the world can you do with music?" "You don't want to be a teacher." I will never forgive myself for having said that.

When he graduated from high school and received a "full-ride scholarship" to the University of Denver, he chose accounting as his major. I'm sure he wanted to make me happy. What a fool I was. No wonder he blew his freshman year in college. He was trying to please his daddy by majoring in accounting. I learned a very difficult and expensive lesson. Never tell your child what he/she should be.

Micheal then went to work at a local fast food restaurant. Later, he launched a model urban 4-H program in Pueblo, Colorado. By that time, he felt ready to return to school, more focused and mature in his goals. He enrolled at the University of Southern Colorado. What an achievement reversal!

Micheal and Pamela's (Thomas) wedding in Columbus, Nebraska, November 1978.

Micheal became a straight "A" student and established close relation-ships with USC faculty members, including Chuck Ford and Dr. Wally Steeley. Steeley was a political science professor and one of the most powerful lobbyists in the state of Colorado. He lobbied for various government entities and banks. This was an incredible hands-on training experience for my son, Micheal.

After receiving his Bachelor of Science degree, Micheal went on to the University of West Florida in Pensacola to receive his Masters degree and later, a degree in law. He continued on to become a senior staff aide to Pueblo U.S. Congressman Ray Kogovsek. For six years, he and his wife, Pamela, lived in Washington, D.C. and Alexandria, Virginia, where his two children were born. At the time of his death, at age 45, Micheal was the Executive Director for the National Association of Social Workers, based in Denver. His death in 1997 was another difficult time in my life, but (again) I am blessed. Micheal's wife, Pamela, was a Godsend. She was there for him and was emotionally supportive not only to Micheal, but also to the family and me.

Several of Micheal's friends served as pallbearers at his funeral. Two of them, former Congressman Ray Kogovsek and Chuck Ford, worked with Mike in Washington D.C. and became close personal friends.

At the funeral service, during the Eulogy, Chuck and Ray had great things to say about Mike and his accomplishments. Congressman Kogovsek spoke directly to Mike's children about the legacy left for them and for all

Colorado citizens. He told Joelle and Gabriel about how their father successfully negotiated and convinced all sides to accept legislation that would protect public lands for the enjoyment of future generations.

About a month after the funeral, I received the following letter from Mike's first cousin, Dwayne Kelly Gonzales (Rudy and Gloria's son). Enclosed with the letter was a poem written by Dwayne Kelly honoring my son.

October 8, 1997
Dear Uncle Bonney and family,

After hearing the testimonial about Mike, I was inspired to write a Poem, about one of his many accomplishments. We had no idea of the type of work in which Mike was involved. Learning about the impact he had on other lives made us very proud to have such a man of integrity in our family. The eulogy regarding his efforts in saving a very large area of the mountains was very moving and truly inspiring. As former Congressman Kogovsek said, "These Mountains are Micheal's legacy," not only to his family, but also everyone who loves and enjoys the Rocky Mountains. As for myself, when I look to the western horizon and see the Rocky Mountain range, I think about Mike. I hope you do not mind that I took the liberty in writing this poem. I hope you enjoy it as much as I loved writing this tribute to him.

Sincerely,
Kelly D. Gonzales

Micheal's Mountains
(Kelly D. Gonzales)

Micheal's Mountains

Climaxing spires dominating the western horizon of the Colorado Rocky Mountains

Eclipsing fiery orange sunsets with vibrant prisms of majesty

Complementing infinite deep aqua skies with radiant greens and serene blues

Exploding with reds, oranges and violets of brilliant mountain wild flowers

>*Blooming with charismatic colors*

Micheal's Mountains

Snowcapped pinnacles saturating the sky with glittering beauty

>*Reflecting the luminating warmth of life-giving sun*

>*Releasing teeming, rolling creeks of refreshing water*

>*Rapidly, yet gently tumbling downward into sparkling crystal clear ponds*

>>*Nurturing the advent of springtime and rebirth of new hopes and dreams*

>>*Of young generations viewing their dawn for the first time*

Among the lush jade grasses and countless emerald trees

Thrive varieties of wildlife,

>*Each bringing vitality to the landscape with their elegant movements*

>>*As they gracefully, effortlessly traverse the mountains*

>>*Caring for their young and gathering food*

Be they foraging ground dwellers, floating among the trees
or navigating the sky
>*Each is unique in character and gift they give to*
>*the forest*
>*And pleasure they reveal to the eye*

Micheal's Mountains,
>*Two million acres of the magnificent Rocky Mountains*
>*Saved for all time by the patient, persuasive efforts of one man*
>*A man who believed in the future, family and God*
>*A man who lived by faith, honesty, trust, loyalty*
>*And courage*

These mountains are Micheal's legacy for everyone
>*An endowment of eternal, elegant beauty*
>*Natures monument to the promise of hope*
>*An agreement to cherish, preserve and protect life that*
>*flourishes in the hills*
>>*So future generations of children can enjoy and*
>>*witness*
>>>*The miracle of life, beauty and natures*
>>>*mysteries*
>>>*Found only in the wilderness of the Rocky*
>>>*Mountains*

The majestic splendor God intended for people to enjoy forever
Peaking at the gates of the paradise of angels
An immense memorial to nature, heaven and the tranquility of
humankind
Summits where peace and happiness are realized
Mountains for an eternity
Micheal's Mountains

My sons Micheal and Jimmy were profiles in courage. Both of them endured incredible ordeals prior to their premature deaths. My son, Micheal, endured incredible physical discomfort prior to his death from diabetes. He had his first of four open-heart surgeries at the age of 30. His vision was impaired and shortly before he died, both of his legs were amputated. On Micheal's 45th birthday, he had a stroke. For the last few months of his life he courageously continued his work, yet confined to his wheelchair.

I still remember the heartbreak we both felt when he failed a driving examination. Self-sufficiency was so important to my son. When the examiner confided in me that Micheal would never be able to transport himself by car again, I was crushed for him.

Diabetes is a cruel, relentless disease. Slowly, day by day, it inexorably strips a person of their dignity and

Jimmy vacationing in New York City, 1984.

Jimmy, with two other Medical students dissecting cadaver at CU Medical school, 1970s.

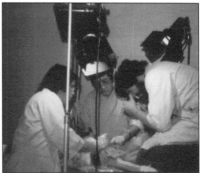

independence, of mobility and of everything that makes them feel autonomous. Vision is lost. Limbs become unusable. Strength is drained and even breathing becomes labored. Diabetes cannot be cured. It can only be endured and when you believe the worst has come, another painful new indicator of debilitation emerges. Micheal though, never, ever stopped trying. So when the call came that he had collapsed while doing his lobbying job at the state capitol, I wasn't surprised.

Thank God, illness was not the only thing in our lives, yet the illness brought our family closer together. We were

Afternoon rafting trip in the Eagle River between Vail and Glenwood Springs. Bonney and Jimmy on right side of raft wearing caps, Jimmy wearing the MEDA cap, July 1983. Jimmy was at doctors' convention in Vail; Bonney was his guest.

Jimmy water skiing with his brothers and sister at Pueblo Reservoir, 1980s.

Jim, Lucille and Ron, Easter Sunday at 113 N. Circle Drive in Canon City, home, 1979.

Bonney, Lucille and Jimmy vacationing in San Francisco, late fall 1984.

there for each other… and never let it dominate our existence. Lucille and I enjoyed growing up with our children. Winters in Fremont County were fun, especially when the children were younger. I enjoyed pulling their sleds behind my Volkswagen bug in the hills around Florence. Later all six of us learned to ski at the Broadmoor Hotel ski area in Colorado Springs. We took numerous weekly excursions to the Monarch ski area, and when we had a little extra money, we skied in Vail or Breckenridge, Colorado. Summers we went camping, fishing… sometimes with other families and friends. Once we took a family trip to Juarez Mexico with my mother. It was her idea… she offered to be our tour guide. The kids never forgot this one. They still talk about it. The boys also never forgot the friendly wrestling matches with their grandpa, Albert. They always looked forward to having "little chicken" (grandpa) visit our home.

In 1996, while Micheal was ill but still working, the University of Denver Graduate School of Social Work honored him for his leadership role as executive director of the National Association of Social Workers (NASW). The University created the Micheal Lopez Scholarship. The scholarship, of $10,000, is funded by the Graduate School and is awarded each year to a second year student who is specializing in Community Practice—leadership, management, and community organizing. The Award reads "Micheal Lopez, therefore, is an excellent role model for the recipients of the award named for him."

My Son Ronnie

While my youngest son, Ronald Lopez, a Colorado Springs Police Fugitive Unit Officer, projects physical strength and confidence, there are as many books as there is weight-lifting equipment in his comfortable home in the northwest part of the city.

When Ronnie graduated from high school, we took him and Jilda on a trip to Jamaica. That was a terrific two-week vacation! We were delayed on our return through Miami because "independent Ronnie" decided that he could get through customs without his parent's help. His full beard and hippie attire nearly landed him in jail.

On his wall are many 65K class championship gold and silver medals for Judo Masters and seniors competitions. Ron has competed in Judo for twenty years. This is an activity that he enjoys with his son and daughter, Joshua and Jennifer. Judo is a blue-collar sport, hard work and you have to be committed to succeed. Ron says, " I picked Judo because you can physically control people without hurting them." He has trained at the nearby U.S. Olympic Center, but if you were to bump into him at K-Mart, you wouldn't think, "Now, here's a cop." Ron isn't a rough Billy Jack type of cop. He smiles easily, for one thing. After work, he doesn't hang around with the other officers. When his dangerous, pressure-filled workday is over, he doesn't unwind at a cop bar. By 5:05 p.m., his car is turning the corner into his driveway or heading into the St. Mary's High School parking lot, where he assists in coaching their wrestling team.

Ron became a member of the SWAT team not long after he joined the Colorado Springs Police Force. The SWAT team had been his lifelong pursuit and he was consumed by his work. Lucille and I were very concerned about his safety, especially when he'd give us the details of his nightly activities.

He was once called to a disturbance at a bar frequented by a rough crowd nearly every night. Ronnie expected trouble because a group of bikers had arrived on the scene and a fight had ensued. At the point when Ronnie approached the commotion, a riot began. Ronnie got out of his police car and asked his partner to call for "back-up" (additional officers). Suddenly Ronnie and his partner had become the enemy. Threats and challenges were directed at them, and the groups that were fighting one another, joined forces against the police and had no intention of letting them inside the bar.

Ronnie said that he asked God for protection and started swinging his baton and began hollering like a maniac. As he walked through the bar, the people parted like the Red Sea, in his estimation. His partner had wanted to wait for back up but Ronnie felt that he needed to make an immediate decision. He felt that if he and his partner had given any appearance of fear (and they were afraid), that they might have been attacked and possibly killed.

When the back up finally arrived, Ronnie was questioned as to how he managed to get inside the building. Before he could answer, one of those arrested responded, saying that he thought that the officer (Ronnie) had 'gone crazy' and was about to start using his weapon against us. It made me sober up, he said."

Another instance involved a middle of the night no-knock entry that ultimately led to a drug-dealing arrest. A man, a woman and a dog were in a dark, back bedroom. When Ron was a few feet away from them, the woman pointed a gun at him and Ron shot her through the chest. Amazingly enough, the woman didn't die but she sued the city, claiming that she thought that she was being robbed, despite the fact that the SWAT team was yelling "Police!" from the moment they entered their house (not to mention their uniforms that clearly read "Police". In the house, the police recovered drugs, drug money and various weapons. Ronnie could write a book about all that happened subsequent to this incident. Had he shot the woman in the head and mortally wounded her, the city would have saved itself a lot of problems.

Ronnie was only five and Jilda was two when we went to the New York World's Fair. Both of them stayed in Alamosa with their Grandparents, Sarah and Albert. We tried to make it sound like they were going on a trip but even at that age they knew they got the raw end of the deal. I guess I felt guilty for not taking them with us so I bought Ronnie a Shetland pony, together with saddle, two-wheeled riding rig and everything that went with it. Jilda insisted on a baby chick. Who would have ever thought that the chick would become a chicken and follow Jilda around, wearing doll clothing.

The pony was well trained, and perfect for children. That pony, "Dynamite", was the kids' and the neighbors' entertainment for almost five years. We just tied the little critter to a special metal post. When we came home at the end of the day he had designed a perfect circle by eating every blade of grass around the post. Next morning we moved the post. In the winter, we got him a few bales of hay and some grain. Everything was going great except we were getting calls from the neighbors and the police that the horse

Ron with his mother in Canon City. He was living in Pueblo, working nights at a Safeway store and attending the University of Southern Colorado full time, 1980.

was in someone's yard or out in the middle of Main street. After consulting with Ron, I sold the horse and everything for $100.00 and told him the money would go in his savings account.

Being the youngest boy, Ronnie had to learn how to handle tricks imposed on him, by his older brothers... mostly gags and jokes. It didn't take long before Ronnie was the one to become their bodyguard. In junior high school, Ron was the biggest football player... other kids looked up to him and wanted to be just like him. He could score a touchdown and carry two opponents with him over the goal line. Ronnie was also the advocate (defender) for the younger and smaller kids in his classes. More than once we received a call from the headmaster (of Holy Cross Abbey) telling us that Ron was being sent home for beating up another kid. Each time, it would turn out that Ron was merely protecting some smaller student from a bully.

As a sophomore in high school, he came home early one day and told me he'd been sent home because he beat up another student (a senior). When Lucille and I arrived at the school office, the headmaster pointed to the senior and said: "Look what your son did to this boy."

"That's impossible, this boy is twice as big as Ron." Lucille said. The kid looked like a truck hit him. As it turned out, the senior had stolen another student's car and intentionally ran into Ron's freshly painted Plymouth. Ron had been working part-time for a local auto dealer and used his earnings to fix up this old car. Ron was expelled for a week but the senior, who came from a wealthy out-of-state family, remained in school. Three months later that senior was expelled for having alcohol in his dormitory room.

One summer, Ronnie went to visit his brother, Mike, in Washington, D.C. I noticed that he was carrying a lot of baggage. I thought, perhaps he intended to stay a long time. It turned out that he was carrying several suitcases full of Pueblo green chile for his brother, Mike. He spent a couple of weeks in Washington and when he came back he said: "I know you and mom want me to get my degree in business, but now I am more convinced than ever that I want to be a peace officer."

After obtaining his degree in business from the University of Southern Colorado, he went on to the police academy. Ron always wanted to be a cop... ever since he was a little boy. Shortly after joining the Colorado Springs Police department, he was asked to join the SWAT team.

Lucille and I would pray for Ron every night. She knew that Ron was working nights and would call him first thing every morning.

Ronnie is not a mean, tough person; rather, he is one of the kindest persons in the world. I've seen him cry; trying to understand why people can be so cruel to one another. He cried like a baby when he stood by watching his brother, Jimmy, die. He loved Jimmy so very much and could not cope with his death.

Mike saw how hard Ronnie was taking the loss of his brother. Once again, he used humor to break the ice. Ronnie, in tears, holding his brother's head, saying, "Oh Mike, he's so cold". Mike responds, "Not over here, Ron, just get closer" As Ron gets closer, Mike grabs Jim's hand and slaps Ronnie across the face with it. Changed the mood immediately… instant laughter. *Pobrecitos mis hijos.*

After Jim died, I took the whole family to Disney World. We had been planning a trip during Thanksgiving holidays, but Jim got sick the first of November and remained in the hospital until he died two months later. We had originally planned a deep sea-fishing trip to Mazatlan, Mexico. The kids didn't want to go there without Jim, so we went to Florida. While in Florida, I could sense that my children were hurting from the loss of their mother and brother. I just wanted to do something to make us all feel better.

Police Academy Graduation in Colorado Springs. Ann, Police Officer Ronald Lopez and Bonney, 1981.

Ronald Lopez:

At the Police Academy twenty-one years ago, my training officer would have gone nuts if I would subdue a person without beating the crap out of them, but that's just not my style. My peers see me working out so hard and ask me why. I tell them that its because I want to compete, because fat cops don't command respect and also for another important reason: I want to stay in shape because of what happened to my brothers, Mike and Jimmy. They died of diabetes. If the disease attacks me the way it did them, I want to fight it as hard as I can. I have a family and I want to stay alive for them.

How I am as a person, father and cop, comes from my dad. My father was always gentle, never spanked us and took time to talk to us. Dad taught me that, as a Hispanic, I would have to work twice as hard and be twice as good. I train a lot, go through all the mental 'what-ifs'. And, I talk to God. Actually, I carry all my family with me when I am on duty.

I can feel God's presence with me. This may sound crazy, but I deal with people the way Jesus would. I don't strip them (arrestees) of their dignity or cuff them in front of their kids. Sometimes when I am down at the jail, I see an old contact, they'll thank me by saying: "Hey, Ron, I remember you. It's nice to see you again. You really treated me well." I tell them that if they want, they can get straightened out and be a good parent.

This is a way of keeping Mom alive, I think. Her faith was paramount in her life. She always left it up to God. "God will put you where he wants you. Leave it to God," Mom always said. I ask myself constantly how Mom would handle a situation and use faith as a tool for living and working. Mom was so beautiful. I knew when her illness was getting worse because the medication she was taking, made her gain weight. At night, I'd see Mom and Dad quietly talking when they didn't think we could hear. I knew that they were concerned. When I got married in 1982, Mom was so sick that we had our wedding in Canon City. Ann's parents insisted upon it.

The best parts of me come from Mom, Mike and Jimmy. When they died, I was filled with anger and couldn't understand why. There was such a loss of joy in my life. For a long time, it was very hard for me. Then I decided to give my children what I'd had, a

Ronald and Ann (Burguete) Lopez wedding in Canon City, June 26, 1982. Wedding party: Jilda, Marquelle (flower girl), Sharon (Ann's sister), Ann, Ronald, Jimmy and Dan (Ann's brother).

great childhood. I couldn't be depressed anymore and dwell on my pain. It would have been a disservice to my kids, to mom and dad and my brothers.

Jimmy gave me his humility. He was a sharp student, an exceptional athlete and a physician. But when he was sick and in the hospital and a janitor would come in to mop the floor, Jimmy would thank them for doing their job and then ask them their name. When I asked him why he did this, he said it was because he'd learned that there comes a time when even the most able person can't do things. He'd introduce himself as Jim, not Dr. Lopez. Jimmy taught me that it is possible to be proud and humble at the same time.

Mike gave me his sense of humor and his kindness. When Mike was sick, he was always so good to my kids. Josh was always on his lap, laughing. He was a helluva guy, so upbeat. Mike would always handle a situation with laughter. Even when Mom and Jimmy died, Mike made us see the joy of life. To Mike, laughter was the best medicine. I am kind of living through Mike now. And Mike lives through me.

Bonney's 69th birthday at his home in Highlands Ranch. Eddie, Bonney, Ronald, and grandsons, Gabriel and Joshua.

My Daughter Jilda

It was Sunday, Mother's Day, May 8, 1960, that Dr. John Buglewicz delivered the last one of our children, the youngest and our only girl. Jilda arrived at the hospital in Florence, Colorado.

Talk about a proud daddy. I quickly announced the event to all the men and boys attending the Boy Scout breakfast at Saint Benedict's parish hall that morning. John Powhida, a Retired Army Colonel, was the guest speaker that day.

Ready for Easter Sunday Mass, Florence, Colorado, 1963.
Ronald, James, Micheal and Jilda

Jilda's brothers immediately took a liking to her and became very protective. In fact, both her parents and brothers began a life-long program of spoiling little Jilda. It was okay for her brothers to tease her and make her cry but if an outsider looked at her crosswise, there'd be hell to pay. "No one touches my sister," they'd say.

Of course, Jilda could not serve as an altar boy as her three brothers did because in those days, girls were not allowed to serve as acolytes in the Catholic Church. She did, however, attend Saint Michael's Catholic school in Canon City from the third through eighth grades. After that, she went on to St. Scholastica Academy, a private girl's school in Canon City, where she graduated in 1978.

Many of Jilda's high school classmates came from foreign countries, since Saint Scholastica Academy was a boarding school. Local students, however, could attend and participate in all school activities. The school was similar to Holy Cross Abbey, where the boys graduated. My children had many friends attending area public schools. It was shared attitude that those in the public

Picnic at Veteran's Park in Canon City, summer 1988. Grandpa Albert, Jilda and Jim.

school arena envied those who were in the private school sector. I was once chastised by a public school principal for sending my children to private schools, "when we have such great public schools here in Florence," he said. I'm sure my children have had similar experiences.

Jilda did very well in school, participated in many school activities and was well liked by classmates and teachers alike. When she was in ninth grade, I suggested she find a part-time job so that she could get some work experience. My boys had all done the same thing while in high school. I believe children should get more than just "book-learning." They must learn the responsibility of holding down a job; regardless of the type of job it might be.

After interviewing at the local Safeway store, Jilda came home crying one afternoon. She said the manager wouldn't hire her because she was too small and wouldn't be able to lift heavy items. You don't say things like that to the child of a Hispanic father-or to any father, for that matter. Before the sun went down on that young Safeway store manager, he had learned a very important lesson from a not-so-inexperienced businessman.

The next day Jilda went to work as a bagger. A few days later I go shopping at Safeway and find my little girl carrying a fifty-pound sack of potatoes out to a customer's car, while a husky young male bagger stands there laughing, watching. I was tempted to confront the manager again, but I controlled myself. The employees and manager gave Jilda all of the "dirty jobs", hoping she would give up and quit. Jilda was determined to prove her abilities in handling any job and this job was no exception.

Within a year Jilda became a checker. Several years later when this same manager acquired his own store, he asked Jilda to help train his new staff. Now, when I see him, he always asks about Jilda... and I thank him.

Years later, my little girl, the one who was too small to work at Safeway, became a great heroine. She volunteered to donate a kidney so that her brother, Jim, might live.

After the kidney transplant, she continued her heroic work, taking the place of her mother, by offering support and encouragement to her brothers whenever they needed it. Now that I live alone, she calls me daily to check on me. She truly has a heart of gold.

Jilda was a normal teenager. She attended dances, had boyfriends, and etc. Her mother, however, was very protective of her and always wanted to know where she went and whom she was with. Many times Jilda was not allowed to go places or be with certain people because her mother did not approve. Today Jilda often tells me that she is so glad her mom was strict with her. She tells me she could've gotten into a lot of trouble had her mom not set such strict rules for her. All of Jilda's boyfriends had to "pass the test" and if they didn't, they were history. I always backed Lucille in her decisions regarding the kids.

One afternoon Lucille called my office and asked me to come home Jilda was having problems with a boy. It seems she had "dumped" this young man, whom none of us liked anyway. The young man had invited himself into our home and was refusing to leave. I arrived at the house and politely asked him to leave. He became belligerent with me so I demanded that he leave my home immediately. He refused but as I walked toward him, he ran out the door shouting obscenities at me. He called me a "dirty f___ing Mexican." That was a big mistake on his part.

University of Denver graduation, May 1982. Jilda and her grade school and college classmate, Patty Camerlo from Florence. Jilda received her Bachelor of Science Degree in Business and Finance. Later she received an advanced degree in Banking.

Jilda had complained to me about this boy the night before, and I called his father about the problem. The father said, "I'm sorry, he's 18 and there's nothing I can do about it". "You'll have to take care of the matter yourself... it's your problem."

I took care of the problem all right. I called the police and filed a restraining order. During the interview, Jilda told them he wanted to hurt her and/or her mother and that he was acting crazy. When the police went to serve the restraining order, they learned that we were right. He was acting crazy. The officers called and told us that, after speaking with him, they felt he needed to be placed under observation at the Colorado State Hospital for the mentally ill. He was committed, for a few days and later released.

When the father learned that his son had been sent to the State Hospital, he called me madder'n a hornet. "Why did you do that to my son?" he asked. "Because you told me it was my problem and you couldn't handle him," I replied. A few days in the "loony bin" taught that boy never to mess with my daughter again. It probably taught the dad a lesson too.

I always spent time with each of my children, alone, so that we could talk about anything. This way, I could devote my time to one child without disruptions from the other three. Often, Jilda and I would take a ski trip to Monarch Ski Resort. Our conversations, while riding the chairlifts, never seemed long enough.

Jilda received a scholarship to attend the University of Denver where she majored in Accounting and Finance. The scholarship didn't pay all her expenses so she worked at various jobs to help pay for her education. One of those jobs was that of a gasoline attendant at Vickers-a quick-service filling station. It was while working there that the president of a local bank met her and asked: "What's a girl like you doing in a place like this?" She was such a tiny lady and she had grease all over her. She told him that she was working to pay for her education at DU (University of Denver). He gave her his business card and told her to contact him at the bank.

This was the beginning of her banking career. She's been a vice-president of a major Denver bank for many years. Recently she informed me that she's retiring after over 25 years. She expresses interest in teaching business classes at DU later on. I know she deserves great things and I pray that she and her new husband, Lee Weinstein enjoy many wonderful years together.

In June 2001, Jilda gave her daddy a surprise 70th birthday party at the Fort Restaurant in Denver.

Lee and Jilda on their cruise to China, October 2002

Jilda Lopez/Weinstein:

Sometimes my father and I will talk about the losses we have had or the trials we've had to endure. We both agree that these painful experiences were, in some ways, a gift and a blessing to our family too. We have learned from the gift of pain. It created a bond between siblings and parent, which remains unshakable. We never had inter-generational separations or lack of understanding that many families seemingly have. Friends were important, yes, but family always came first.

Mom always insisted on dinner together. We'd tease her that food to her was a way of counseling us. We always prayed before partaking of any meal-even a sandwich. At the table, we could talk about anything we wanted without fear of censure. We were always on the same page-knew what our priorities were.

We were in a battle together and the enemy was diabetes. The enemy was assaulting my brothers and it had to be held at bay. We became each other's caretakers. Protective of each other at all times. In effect, I became a third parent, assuming responsibilities beyond those any child should have to shoulder. Yet, I do not feel as though my childhood was stolen from me. Mom and Dad always let us be kids too.

All of us cherished mom. She was truly beautiful and radiated. I have such fond memories of my mother. Her touch was powerful, just a stroke of our hair and we melted in her arms. My relationship with her continued to grow with our "girl talks". Because she was sick, I often found her resting on the couch or in her bedroom. I would join her and we would talk for hours. She told me how difficult it was for her after her mother died. As a child this was difficult to understand but now I do understand.

When I was four (or five) years old, Micheal often babysat me. Once, while he was baby sitting, I was in the living room and heard a loud thump in the next room. Running to the kitchen, I found him in convulsions. I was just a child, but I knew what to do, so I first called an ambulance than my parents. We looked out for each other. Nothing was going to hurt my brothers. Yes, sometimes they took advantage of their naive little sister, as older brothers normally do. They used dark, self-deprecating humor to deal with it. Laughter became the "doctor" within us, a tool we learned to manipulate with skill.

At my Dad's 70th birthday party (June 2, 2001) I said to those celebrating with us how "the world is not going to remember us as MDs, CPAs, Peace Officers or Bankers but as a family." We are a family that is loyal to one another, no matter what.

Jimmy and I shared a home for ten years. We were like a couple, yet it wasn't perfect having a brother as a roommate. We dated and had an active social life. But sometimes it was just he and I dealing with stuff. We cried together, we'd fight, then we'd make up and go out to dinner. We were closer than close. I recall once (for some reason) my mom was going to spank me. I ran to Jim for protection. "Mom don't spank her, she didn't mean it, hit me instead" he pleaded. How were we to know that this small incident would bring us to such closeness for the rest of our lives? It was meant to be and God had a hand in how we needed to be there for each other. Jimmy found me crying in my bedroom once. He knew I was hurting. He stroked my back and said "Jilda, you need to know something... I will always love you, even if you fail." Please understand that your family will always support you, no matter what."

I still miss him... I learned so much about life from him.

Mike and I were eight years apart, so I was always his baby sister, who sometimes got in the way. I would do anything Mike asked. Since I was the only girl, I had my own bedroom. The three boys shared a bedroom, bunk beds and all. Mike told me I was missing out on all the fun and convinced me to let him have my bedroom.

After Jim died, I got to know Mike better and we got closer to each other. I spent much time with him at the hospital. We began sharing our lives and remembering our life with Jimmy. The hardest

Bonney and daughter, Jilda Lopez/Weinstein at her wedding in Hawaii, January 2002.

thing for me was that I knew Mike was watching himself die through Jimmy. Everything that happened to Jimmy was now happening to him. Mike did not fear death… but he knew that he was going to leave his children and it was ripping his guts out. He responded by spoiling the heck out of both kids; letting them know he loved them. He held his head high and lived his life out with dignity.

Jimmy's illness and eventual death was a shock, especially after losing our mother only two years earlier. With Mike, I knew what was going on and what to expect. The slow, but inevitable stages of debilitation were no surprise… just a nightmare revisited. The last few months of his life, we called each other every night and spent much time together. The last time I visited with him in the hospital we talked of the inevitable and he thanked me for being a part of his life

Ron has a special place in my heart. I watched him grieve for our brothers and mom. It seemed to consume him and broke my heart. I couldn't take his pain away. But Ron has gotten through it and has become a wonderful person and father. I know mom would have been so proud of him.

Dad became the biggest worry.. There are things and events that he probably doesn't remember now. He shut down, became the "details" person, hid behind the tasks of taking care of things, of others and making arrangements for funeral services. When Micheal died, I'd called Dad to tell him that his son, my brother, was gone from us. Yet, when Dad came to the hospital and approached Mike's bed and said, "Hito, how are you?" His pain was so acute that he could not accept the death of his son-not yet.

He had to shut down. Dad had been so strong for the rest of us that he couldn't bear his own pain.

My dad and I have a special relationship. Maybe its because I'm still his "little girl" or its because we have experienced so much together, but I could have not asked for a better father. When I was small he instilled in me that I was capable of achieving all of my dreams. I can honestly say my success and work ethic can be attributed to my father. One of dad's best qualities is how giving he is. He will not only give of himself to love you but he will give to total strangers because they are in need. I remember my father saying that he has been blessed threefold because of one small act of kindness. I have watched him over the years live by this, daily.

MY BEST FRIENDS

Eddie and Gloria

I was the oldest of three children born to Albert and Sarah (Jiron) Lopez. My brother, Eddie, is a year and a half years younger and my sister, Gloria, is seven years younger than I am. Ours has always been a very close relationship.

When my parents were living, our family reunions occurred often. After they died, the three of us continued our get-togethers. As years passed our individual families grew larger, yet the bond between us three grows stronger. We don't need a special occasion to have a reunion. A simple get-together always turns into a festive occasion… that's how much we enjoy each others company. As the years go by, the more festive occasions we have.

My sister, Gloria (Lopez) Gonzales and husband Rudy Gonzales on their 30th wedding anniversary. Married at St. Augustine's Catholic Church in Antonito, Colorado December 26, 1955.

My brother, Eddie and JoAnn (Ortega) Lopez on their 50th wedding anniversary.

Growing up in San Antonio, Eddie and I enjoyed raising orphaned lambs (commonly referred to as *"pencos"*). Lambing time occurred every spring at my Grandpa Luis' ranch and there were always plenty of *pencos* to be raised. We didn't know it but this was kind of like a 4-H program. After the lambs were old enough they were returned to the herd. I never got to show them or sell them. But feeding them milk with a pop bottle and nipple was fun. We competed at raising the best looking *pencos*.

Because we didn't have many toys, our grandparents would teach us to build our own. I recall a wind-up toy made of a thread spool, nail, rubber band and a three-inch long stick. Notches cut on the sides gave the toy more traction. When you wound it up, the toy would move along the floor for short distances. We'd spend hours with my grandfather building these contraptions. Then we'd race them to see who had built the fastest one.

Another toy was a rim off a wagon (or other farm equipment). The rim had to be lightweight enough so it could be pushed along with a wire fashioned into a handle. The handle would serve as the guide to steer the wheel in any direction. We'd push the rim up and down hills or in and out of ditches. The idea was to run fast, guide the rim with the wire, then bring it to an abrupt stop. This toy could keep us running all day. Perhaps this was why we had so many good runners in school.

It seems like every kid in the community had to own *"zankos"* (stilts), especially during spring or late fall when you couldn't go anywhere without stepping in mud puddles. We built them out of two wood slats; two pieces of old leather straps and four nails. The *zankos* could be any length, depending on how high off the ground you wanted to be. The longer the stilt, the longer strides—and the harder the fall. If we didn't have materials to build the stilts, we'd take two empty evaporated milk cans laid side ways, step on them and smash the edges so the can would fasten tightly to the shoe. These cans wouldn't necessarily keep our shoes completely out of the mud puddles but it was better than having no stilts at all. Our parents didn't like these contraptions because clamping them to our shoes often damaged the shoe.

It was not unusual to see boys walking to and from school on their homemade *zankos*. At school, we kept them in a special place where other kids couldn't touch them. We treasured those zankos as if they were expensive bicycles. Of course, no one in the community owned a bicycle at the time.

We attended different schools after we moved to Alamosa. Eddie and Gloria registered at Boyd grade school and I attended junior high school (seventh/eight grades) located in the high school building across town. My brother and I managed to spent weekends and after school hours together, even though we were not in the same grade. I skipped a grade in San Antonio and graduated ahead of friends my own age (Sixteen). Eddie and I, however, enjoyed the same school buddies (Ralph Tabeling, Leroy Romero, Pete Garcia, Amos Cordova, Leo Muniz and Toby Garcia "Bebo Jones") through out my high school years.

Shortly after graduation we went our separate ways. I married Lucille Marquez, Eddie married Joan Ortega, and Gloria married Rudy Gonzales. I'm the only one to leave *el Valle* (the San Luis valley), however.

Eddie and Gloria (and Joan and Rudy) remained close to my parents and assisted them in their old age. Gloria cared for my mother until her final days then she cared for my father until his death a year later. Eddie kept my father busy by taking him fishing and creating work for him in his business. He also saw that my mother was comfortable and provided for her needs, including a rent-free apartment.

Because I was away, I missed many of those enjoyable times with my elderly parents. Now when we get together, they tell me about those days. Some are sad experiences but most are lively and humorous stories about my parents.

Eddie and Joan are always busy with their children and grandchildren and their businesses. But let anyone in the family have a need and they're right there to lend a hand. I can't count the number of times they have been there to give me moral support. Like when I was in court (the lawsuit), and I was going through a very difficult time. It seemed friends and family had abandoned us, but Joan and Eddie were right there. Eddie was there again when Jimmy was having a kidney transplant in Minneapolis. Lucille and I were there alone with Jim and Jilda, both in the hospital, when who shows up to give us moral support, but my brother Eddie. After Lucille left us, I was faced to deal with both my sons and their illness, without help or encouragement from their mother. Yet, Eddie and Joan were there to help. Time and time again, without my asking for help, my sister in-law Joan would show up and stay with my boys so that we (Jilda, Pam and I) could get some rest. When the boys lost their appetite and couldn't eat the hospital foods, she cooked them the old fashioned foods for the sick (*remedios-atole and poliadas*). It never failed, she'd nurse them back to better health. Words cannot explain how much I appreciate the help and support they have given me.

During these difficult times, Eddie and I began to discuss and share our feelings, hurts and emotions. We began to heal our pain by talking about our losses, for he too had lost his only son at an early age.

This Lopez family always seems to deal with tragedy by focusing on humor and the good things in life. Just like Micheal engaged us in laughter (humorous stories and jokes to uplift our spirits) when Lucille died and again when Jim died, Eddie does the same. Eddie and I began traveling everywhere and anywhere, on a moment's notice. Trips to Mexico, New York, New Mexico, you name it. He helped prevent me from getting into a state of depression and it worked.

Eddie, Rudy and I continue to schedule hunting and fishing excursions months, sometimes years in advance.

Pat Comiskey

A lthough I am an accountant, a CPA capable of solving extremely complex problems for corporate clientele, I am still very given to doing business with a simple handshake. My word is my bond as it was for those who preceded me. It was with a handshake that I contracted with Pat Comiskey to join his accounting firm soon after Lucille's death. I became the "Rainmaker" (an expression given to those who bring in the "rain" to a business i.e., as rain is to a drought) to market his accounting practice in 1988.

Pat Comiskey tending his horses at the Comiskey Ranch near Westcliffe, Colorado, 1999.

Patrick Comiskey had worked for me as a junior accountant when he first graduated from college. From the first day, I saw a brilliant young man with exceptional potential. My assessment of him was correct. Soon thereafter, he passed the CPA exam with high scores. We've been good friends ever since.

Pat is the same age as my oldest son, Mike. I

Pat at his Denver office, 1988.

always wanted to have a son who would follow in my footsteps and take over my accounting practice. Since none of my children chose accounting as a profession, I felt that Pat was my "son" the one who would take over my accounting practice someday. What is more amazing is that our friendship over the years has remained steadfast and because of the bond that has developed, I truly consider him my son.

Over the years I've learned that unless one has good communication skills, it is easy to lose effectiveness, regardless of technical knowledge. Within six months after passing the CPA exam, I signed up to take several self-improvement courses, including, but not limited to, the Dale Carnegie and Toastmasters courses. Most importantly, I've learned to listen and to watch others. It's surprising how much knowledge you cultivate by sitting back and simply listening. You gain control and respect of others by fully understanding those around you. I've also learned that it is important to speak only when I have something of consequence to say and to only take credit for my own ideas. Only after putting yourself in a client's shoes can you understand their needs and give them advice. I see myself in my friend, Pat Comiskey.

Patrick Comiskey:

Bonney gave me my first job, hired right out of USC (University of Southern Colorado) in 1974. I was really a very shy, worse than rough around the edges rookie and I didn't have an ounce of social skills. I had this fear of dealing with client expectations. Bonney taught me how to be more at ease and refused to let me hide behind a cubicle. How he dealt with me was pretty amazing. It's like he can forecast the finished product, what kind of person you're going to end up being. I worked for him for four years before I got restless and moved on.

Bonney is like a father figure to me. When I worked for him, he made me and all the other staff members feel valued and respected. There are some accounting firms that treat a new employee like dirt; like chattel. It's not that way with Bonney. The way I run my business is a reflection of how Bonney ran his. We are professional and serious, yes, but if you're doing work in the office, we do not require a suit or a tie.

Bonney, though, likes to wear a suit. His duties do require him to be out in the public eye more yet it's a matter of style, I think. He's just a classy guy. He always seems to gravitate toward governmental type contacts. Since he sat on the city council in Florence, he has an edge in that forum. He knows the lingo, so to speak. Certain kinds of clients need to be courted in a very careful, professional fashion. Favoritism is frowned upon yet these clients want to feel important. Bonney fits in just as well with the private contractor clientele. He is just so adaptive and can fit into any crowd. He says, "There you are," not "Here I am."

I have had the sense about Bonney that he never has had a need to enhance his self-image at the expense of another. He has a quiet confidence about him. I believe that the respect he accords to others comes from how he was raised. His family worked in the fields doing a lot of manual labor. This is the same work ethic and dignity that is reflected in his work-that there are no small jobs, only small people.

Bonney has also helped me with many serious personal and family matters. He is always the first person that I would call or go into the office on the weekend to discuss anything that might be on my mind, without ego or pretense.

Bonney, as usual is in his suit and I am in my cowboy boots.

Dr. John V. Buglewicz

L ucille and I were quite fortunate to have many good friends. We became involved socially with people because of commonly shared attitudes and perspectives of life. Our family time was precious to us and the relationship that we fostered amongst friends was an important extension of the values that our family embraced.

The friends that my children chose were never conditioned by the size of their bank account. We expected our children's friends to be well mannered and have a sense of purpose or direction. Some of the kid's best friends were from poor Mexican-American families. Other friends

John and Doris Buglewicz at Bonney's birthday party in Highlands Ranch, Colorado, June 2001.

included children and grandchildren of established community founders.

I, of course, had my political allies. Some of these were new business associates who later became friends. If we spent any time with someone, it was definitely because we really liked them. Just as my brother Eddie and his wife Joann are our oldest and dearest friends, so, too, are John and Doris Buglewicz.

Throughout the years, without a doubt, our most consistently long-term and supportive non-family friends were John and Doris Buglewicz. Our friendship with John and Doris spanned nearly half a century. John has been a rock-solid friend through many triumphs and tragedies. Like myself, John was a widower. Donna, his first wife died at an early age, leaving him, a busy young doctor, with seven small children to raise. One of the children was a mere infant. Doris had also lost her husband and was widowed with two boys of her own, the same ages as two of John's boys.

Well-meaning friends of theirs arranged a date between them, despite their reluctance to play matchmaker to these large

Bonney riding camel in Morocco, North Africa, while touring with Lucille, John and Doris, May 1985.

broods. Friends feared that Doris would lose her sanity at the prospect of falling in love with John and having to raise nine children. However, within three months of meeting, the couple married. Doris converted to Catholicism and I was asked to be her baptism sponsor. On the mantelpiece in their Dillon home rests a great photograph of all eleven members of their family-John, Doris and kids, smiling at the altar.

What I love about this wonderful couple is how they beautifully blended two families into one. Another photograph shows the kids as adults and it is impossible to tell which siblings are biological kin to each parent. They all look so much alike. They are handsome, attractive and confident. Whenever John and Doris speak about a forthcoming graduation (such as for my godchild, Carol), there is no mention of the "biological" parent. To them, it simply does not matter.

John and Doris are at a point in their marriage where they tend to finish each other's thoughts and sentences. John and Doris are kindred spirits of mine; an integral and ongoing part of my life. As a doctor, John was there during the entirety of Lucille's illness. He gave Lucille and I his affection as well as medical treatment. His involvement was more than clinical. For decades, we celebrated, traveled, played politics and invested in financial ventures together. When Lucille was near death, we chose to invite these dear friends of ours on a final trip to Spain.

A friend is someone who knows your strengths and weakness and loves you because of them-not in spite of them.

I truly believe that they care for me unconditionally. God blessed Lucille and I when He brought this family into our lives.

John and Doris:

Doris: *Lucille was the glue that kept us all together. Bonney and John were busy in their careers.*

John: *Lucille came to the hospital with stomach pain, with what appeared to be a gall bladder attack. A biopsy showed her liver to be badly damaged with cirrhosis. The diagnosis was "Primary Bilateral Cirrhosis." This was so very surprising, since there was no history of hepatitis or heavy drinking. Lucille never abused alcohol. It was just bad luck.*

They put her on a regime of steroids. Highly toxic reactions caused her to gain weight, become jaundiced and had other negative effects. They could only slow the progression of the disease, though.

As Lucille became sicker, Jilda tried to assume her role, even to trying to make some of her favorite dishes.

On our trip to Mexico, as usual, Bonney kept getting lost. He'd put himself in harms way just to explore something, once he was even robbed at gunpoint. Bonney just doesn't know a stranger.

He is one of a kind. Lucille kept him on the straight and narrow and let him know when he was going off limits. Lucille was gentile, but she did not tolerate a lot from Bonney.

Doris: *In Florence, some Hispanics resented Lucille and called her "uppity."*

Yet, she would never turn her face to anyone—no matter whom she was with.

Lucille was a good businesswoman, perhaps more conservative than Bonney, who is inclined to take more high risk chances. Her idea was to grow the profit slowly by a measured "make it, keep it" philosophy. They built their wealth together.

John: *We were very closely lined in the lawsuit. I was involved in the same bank owned by the plaintiff who caused Bonney his problems and we, too, were considering a lawsuit against him. I delivered Jilda and met Lucille on a medical house call to their home on North Pike's Peak.*

Jimmy knew what was going to happen to him. They were ten years ahead of their time, medically speaking. Thirty years ago we didn't have "Ace inhibitors." There are so many treatments now which could have saved Lucille's life. A transplant, so common now, could have saved her.

It just seemed as though this was a family under a cloud. Yet, there was so much joy there, too.

After Lucille died, Bonney could not be consoled.

We think that is why he dated so much and partied too much after Lucille died.

We never grew apart, but there were times when we felt uncomfortable with what he was doing at the moment. He has been in mourning for a long time.

We think he is finally finding peace.

All the kids were exceptional, but Jimmy was the star — so certain of his goals. Ron took longer to find his own way, and maybe felt pressure to be like the others, but he is doing really well and being his own man. Ron was so much like Bonney in terms of character and strength — if not in career but in attitude — that sometimes Bonney took longer to understand him. They even walk the same. Bonney is proud of him, certainly.

Jilda became a fine person and Michael achieved his unique status.

**Lucille, Doris and John Buglewicz at the
Lopez home in Canon City, 1970**

**Vacationing in Spain with the Buglewicz's-May 1985.
John, Doris, Lucille and Bonney**

LA POLÍTICA

How It Started

My involvement in politics began when I was teaching at Florence High School and active in the Colorado Federation of Teachers. Most of the union members were Democrats. As a local a union organizer, it seemed only logical that I should join the "party of the day." My grandparents and great grandparents were all Republicans. During the depression, my father worked for WPA and my parents believed Franklin D. Roosevelt was the "President of the working People" I too, registered Democrat.

In 1956, I established my accounting business and it didn't take long to realize that most of my new clients were Republican. I quickly learned that Fremont County has a strong Republican populace. It was my desire to be the independent auditor for the County of Fremont, the City of Canon, the City of Florence and a number of government entities.

A good friend, Ray Harward (Fremont County Attorney), suggested I get involved in business activities that would allow me to meet business people involved in local government. He also said "if you want to do business in Fremont County, it won't hurt if you join the Republican

Party." Shortly thereafter, I switched parties and became active in the Republican Party. Before long, I was the auditor for practically every governmental entity in the county and began specializing in governmental auditing/consulting. As a Hispanic businessman in an all white-Anglo business community, I knew that few, if any, business people would suddenly beat a path to my door. If I wanted my business to grow, I would have to mingle with business people and make myself known in places where they socialize. Once I began doing this, both Democrats and Republicans began doing business with me. From this point on it really didn't matter if I remained active in either party. I realized I just needed to gain their confidence and provide professional accounting/tax services. I had the professional expertise and my clients knew I could help them improve their profits.

Everything seemed to be going along perfectly until I attempted to join a couple of service clubs and lodges in the area. I was quickly reminded of my Spanish surname and the color of my skin. It was no surprise that I discovered that Canon City had once been a habitation for the KKK (Ku Klux Klan). It was not that long ago that crosses were burned in the front yard of "undesirables." I personally witnessed a cross burning in the front yard of a family I knew across the street from the high school in Canon City.

My accounting business prospered. By now, Lucille and I were heavily involved in the real estate investment business. She was active in the local country club; church activities and she played duplicate bridge as well as tennis. Our children were doing great in school, well on their way towards college. I thought that I had things under control, but God had other plans for me.

One night, my son, Micheal, called me at 3:00 a.m. Because of the hour we thought that he had been hurt or was in some kind of trouble. Micheal had been working as a Page at the State Capitol.

"Dad, I just want to let you know that I'm changing my political affiliation. I'm becoming a Democrat and I'm going to work on the "Ray Kogovsek campaign for congress," he said.

"Why the hell are you calling me in the middle of the night to tell me that? You do as you please. You're old enough. I need to go back to sleep," I answered. Well, Mike did as he pleased and went on to work in Washington, D.C. with Ray for the next six years.

Of course, Mike had a different agenda when he called that night. He knew that I was a Republican but wanted me to support the Kogovsek for Congress initiative. It didn't take long for my son to convince me. I remembered "Colonel" Fabrizio had told me years before. Quote Mr. Fabrizio "unless you want to run for political office, avoid total commitment to one party." And so I (a Republican) jumped on the Democrat for Congress campaign.

During the campaign, three Fremont County Republicans met one night and decided to form an organization known as "Republicans for Kogovsek."

Kogovsek's opponent for congress was a long-term state senator, who had represented Fremont County for years. The three organizers: myself, Charlie Fry, Canon City's mayor and Tom Camerlo, an influential Florence dairyman, took it upon themselves to plan a fundraiser and invite every citizen in the county-regardless of political affiliation.

A twenty thousand square foot milk barn in Florence served as the place for the fundraiser. It was held on a Saturday night from 6 p.m. to midnight. We had a live band, free beer, a whole roasted pig and lots of free food. There were posters promoting the election of local Democrats as well as Republicans. We gave out free hats promoting Kogovsek for congress. The whole county showed up.

Before the activities began, the chairman of the county Democratic Party confronted me at the entrance to the barn and asked, "What do you mean by putting up posters for Dr. Buglewicz and those Republican candidates? This is a democratic fundraiser for the democrat Ray Kogovsek and other democrats. Take them down," he said.

Josephine Rivera, a staunch Democrat and friend of Republican Dr. Buglewicz was busy putting up the Republican posters. I answered, "Go ahead and take them down. Here's my $450.00 bill for the beer. I'll bring you several other bills from the Canon City mayor and the dairyman for another $1,500.00. You pay for this and it's your party." He walked away and said nothing more.

Ray Kogovsek defeated his opponent and went on to serve as U.S. Congressman in Washington D.C.

Not long afterwards, Governor Richard Lamm, a democrat, appointed me to the "Advisory Committee to the Colorado Property Tax Administrator;" a new committee created by the Colorado legislature. A requirement of serving on the committee was to undergo an oral interview given by a senate committee of about four or five members. Upon meeting the criteria of the committee, you're recommended to the full legislative body for final approval. It was during this committee inquiry that my State representative (Senator) interjected his opinion. Though he was not a member of this committee, he made objections, stating that he wanted to oppose my appointment. He said that he represented Fremont County, the same county where I came from and that he didn't think I should be appointed to the committee. He went on to say that the committee was comprised of three Republicans, three Democrats and that he didn't know what I represented (i.e., what political party I represented). I looked around and saw white-haired men and they all looked very conservative to me. I knew that my fate was sealed. My representative went on, "Had it not been for this man, we would have a Republican representing us in Congress today." He sat down and the committee chairman continued questioning me.

"Mr. Lopez, were you recommended by your county Republican Central Committee for this appointment?"

I answered: "No."

"Well, how were you informed of this duty?"

"Sir, the Governor's office called and asked if I would

accept the appointment and I said yes," I replied.

"What do you have to say about your representative's comments, Mr. Lopez?"

I took a few moments to think of what to say. Then, as if an answer from above, the words came: "I wish my grandparents were still alive because they would have been so proud of their grandson who single-handedly elected a congressman".

The next day I was quoted in the Denver newspapers and so was my representative. One paper quoted him saying: "Once bitten by a WASP, I don't return for more." Another newspaper read "State Representative… refers to Lopez as a WASP." Comments to me by friends in the community abounded. Comments such as "Lopez, the White Anglo Saxon Protestant." Someone even went so far as having election buttons printed up reading: "Lopez the WASP" and "Mr. and Mrs. WASP" and then distributed them in Canon City.

In spite of all the ridiculous objections and grand stand tactics, the full senate confirmed my appointment and I served in this capacity for two terms.

Current Involvement

I continue my involvement in local politics, even today. Shortly after moving to Denver, I was invited to serve on an advisory committee to Mayor Wellington Webb. Later, Mayor Webb appointed me to serve as trustee to the Denver Employees Retirement Plan - a one and a half billion-dollar pension fund. I am currently Chairman of the Board.

I also serve on the Board of Directors and am active in a couple of committees of the CCA (Colorado Contractors Association). This organization is active in Colorado politics and, of course, provides substantial financial support. At election time, CCA and its members, will recommend a slate of officials they want elected to the various state offices.. Both Republican and Democrat candidates are invited to present their political agenda at an all-member meeting. At this particular meeting, a committee had already prepared a slate of candidates to recommend to the full membership.

Kenneth Salazar, a Democratic candidate for State Attorney General, was invited to speak before the membership along with his opponent and other candidates running for state offices. The names of all candidates to be supported (all Republicans) were listed (printed) except for the name of the person to be recommended for State Attorney General. Talk was, the Republican candidate would be added to the list and submitted to the full membership as their recommendation.

After his presentation, Ken Salazar asked me if I knew that a special committee was meeting immediately afterward to make their choices and recommendations. I said, "No." He said, "Could you get me in to talk to the committee?"

I told him that I was not a member of that committee but I'd ask if I could say a few words on his behalf. I made my short presentation than asked if Mr. Salazar could come in and say a few words. It could have been embarrassing to refuse my request at this point; besides, what could they lose? I imagine the committee had already made up their minds.

Ken gave an outstanding presentation. I could see he was gaining support from two key members on the committee. When he left the room, I stayed to hear the discussion that followed. I assume the discussion was not completely open because I was sitting there... but they were not about to ask me to leave.

The results: Two key members spoke in favor of Ken Salazar and convinced all but one person. He was endorsed and I was asked to give him the good news. As we now know, Ken is the first Hispanic to win a statewide election since Colorado's statehood began. I believe that Ken will be our governor before too long.

MY LIFE AS A CPA

Adventures in
Government Auditing

B efore becoming a CPA my friends and I would refer to accountants as bean counters, pencil pushers or green shaded introverts found in a corner sitting on a stool. Never did I imagine that being an accountant could be so exciting. That is, if you want it to be exciting. For that matter, I suppose you can make any job exciting if you really enjoy it.

During my life as an auditor, I've been directly involved in fraud investigations that you would think were made for movies. Such was an initial audit of a Colorado county Department of Social Services in the late 70s which later resulted in the Director going to prison for several years. The media involvement and the behind the scene politics could out do a cop movie.

Another such investigation occurred in the late 80s and early 90s when county commissioners of another county engaged us to investigate the financial activities of the county pension plan. Here too, there was heavy media involvement but the behind the scene politics were even worse. In the midst of the controversy a long-term, popular, elected, official resigned. The charismatic director of the pension plan eventually landed in prison and is still serving time.

Then there was the burning of the historic Conejos County Courthouse on June 27, 1980. We had just completed the annual county audit and presented our reports to the county commissioners (Dale Sowards, chairman, Joe Casias and Ranger Duran). It was three o'clock the following morning when Dale called me at home in Canon City. He was crying and said, "Bonney, our courthouse is on fire. I can see the flames from here." Dale lives approximately ten miles from the courthouse.

Just a few days earlier, we had placed the county financial records (used in the audit) in the large heavy-duty vault located on the second floor of the courthouse and next to the county clerk's office. That same day,

Conejos County Courthouse before and during the fire that destroyed it. Conejos, Colorado, June 1980.

before leaving, we made a physical inspection of all the offices, including the county assessor's where we talked to Danny Trujillo, the Assessor and his assistant Geraldine Romero. The County Health Nurse office had just been moved to the first floor where the county jail had previously been located. The two people working there, Pearl Montoya and Cathy Salazar, were so proud of their newly decorated office. They had only been there a little over a week. The heavy vault came crashing down to the first floor.

When we returned for a subsequent audit, we located many of the records salvaged from the vault but every thing else in the various offices was burned to a crisp. Some of the files we worked on were badly charred and in some cases unreadable. According to Andrew Perea, the present County Clerk, there were two different stories (rumors) floating around about how and why the fire started. Neither story or rumor was ever proven or substantiated.

Consulting Engagement
in Honduras

Then there is the Honduras story in the late sixties—
another "pencil pusher's" project. It seems that the U.S.
government, through the AID program, was looking for
Spanish speaking consultants to provide professional
services to Honduran government elected and appointed
officials. To this day I do not know why I was asked to serve
on this six-week engagement.

John Rosales, a Pueblo college professor/city
councilman, Joe Lontin, Denver city planner, and myself, a
Pueblo/Canon City CPA were selected for the trip. The
purpose of the engagement was to expose these folks to
current government "hands-on" practices used in the United
States. We later learned that the purpose was actually a public
relations effort to support the government in power at the
time.

Several incidents of what seemed to be communist
attempts to overthrow or make changes in the government
were clearly evident. Participants in our workshops consisted
of highly educated individuals as well as individuals who
could not read or write (illiterate). While we were in the

country, the vice president of the United States visited Tegucigalpa, the Capital of Honduras.

I came back from this engagement with much more knowledge and a better understanding of our neighbors and friends in Central America. The teacher learned more from his students than the students learned from the teacher. This was one of the most valuable experiences in my life. It certainly was not a boring "pencil pushing" activity for this accountant.

Joe Lontin:

The first thing I noticed about Bonney is that he would never, ever stay where he belonged.

Bonney and John Rosales from Pueblo accompanied me on a trip to South America. I expected Bonney to act like a "suit" - to be quiet and sort of sink into the background. I soon learned that this was not Bonney's style. We were flying down there on a turbo prop plane and when I looked around for Mr. Lopez, he was nowhere to be found. I went forward to the pilot's cabin and found Bonney sitting in the copilots chair.

"And what does this thingy do?" he asked the pilot. I swear that in the five minutes I watched him, he had asked enough questions to land the damn plane himself.

Once we got on the ground, it was the same thing. We were supposed to be on a public relations AID mission, but the reality was that some locals were not thrilled about having us there.

Bonney, though, was always straying. A trip to the market or festival was cause for me to fear that he had been kidnapped. I'd turn around for a moment and he was gone. After an hour of frantic searching, I would find him engaged in an animated conversation with a local craftsman, doctor or engineer.

Bonney is just so intellectually curious-almost nosey. He didn't really care how much the government paid him to go down there. He was there on a different sort of mission-to learn everything he could.

After the trip to Honduras, I didn't see Bonney for years but I would bet my best riding boots that he had probably applied the lessons he learned from that little dinky trip many times over in his life. I'm not surprised that he is a financial success. He absorbs

Joe and Carmella Lontin enjoying their new boat at Chatfield lake near my home in Highlands Ranch, summer 2000.

people the same way that he absorbs information.

Just recently, Bonney came back into my life. Out of the blue, he tracked me down and continues to be there, as my supporter. The most telling, defining thing that I can say about Bonney is that he is a "collector." Nothing escapes his scrutiny. He collects people, facts and experiences.

I think that Bonney is a generous man and I can't see him using information to hurt anyone. However, if there is an honest business advantage to be gained, he will gain it.

Don't ever take Bonney for granted and just go by appearances.

An Assault on My Character

N ever have I been tested more than when a former employee sued me for defamation of character. This accounting involves betrayal, loss of faith and slander-an out-and-out attack on my professional reputation. This was to be a true test of my moral fiber. According to the Canon City Daily Record newspaper, this notorious lawsuit was among the top ten Fremont County stories for 1982 and was the longest-ever civil trial in county history. Regrettably, this lawsuit named me as the defendant.

The civil suit, described above, was brought about by a former business associate (an ex-employee whom I'll refer to as "John Doe"). Mr. Doe had filed an $8 million grievance suit accusing me of defamation of character and infliction of emotional damage. These damages were extraordinary! From my perspective, his case was totally without foundation and was a brutal character assassination aimed at me.

In short, the man that I'd hired in 1972 seemed to be out to ruin me and obliterate from public memory every single bit of civic good and professional service I had ever performed. For six long weeks, his team of lawyers had relentlessly berated me with their accusations of deceit and libel. They charged me with seeking to defame the integrity of John Doe, who had once been an employee in our accounting firm. I had been a senior partner in this firm for almost twenty years. My integrity, honor and character were at stake, and I fought fiercely to maintain the highest of professional standards while boldly telling the truth.

The jury found me innocent of all charges after scrutinizing over 37 expert witnesses and thousands of legally submitted documents. What the media failed to reveal to the public, however, was the real basis for the lawsuit: racial bigotry and discrimination.

This intolerance was not limited to Mr. John Doe, but also involved a "senior member" of the court system. On September 7, 1982, this senior member of the court system offered his opinion in my case. Testimony revealed he was attempting to unduly influence the presiding judge's opinion against me.

An example of this bigotry and discrimination came from the testimony that was given by police officer John J. Kurtz, Jr. at the trial:

Question: "Now, Officer Kurtz, have you ever heard Mr. John Doe make any statements regarding Mr. Lopez?"

Answer: "Yes sir, numerous times."

Question: "And Officer Kurtz, could you tell the jury what that statement was?"

Answer: "Yes, Mr. Doe stated that he was going to get that blankety-blank Mexican and that he was going to make that blankety-blank Mexican sorry that he ever heard of John Doe. And he said that several times."

Additional testimony given by Stanley Allen Vancil further indicates the racial bigotry that was a theme throughout the trial:

Question: "At any time when you worked at McDonald-Halbig, did you work with John Doe?"

Answer: "Yes, I did".

Question: "Okay, during that time period, did you ever hear Mr. John Doe say anything derogatory about Mr. Lopez?"

Answer: "Yes, I did."

Question: "Would you tell me what that was, please, sir."

Answer: "He said, 'Some day I'm going to get that Mexican.'"

On November 10, 1982, the jury (five women and one man) unanimously found in my favor on a first ballot. However, the jury's ultimate decision did not diminish the anguish and nightmarish experience that I endured. And, to make matters worse, the ordeal only enhanced the pain and physical distress that my wife, Lucille was experiencing as she entered the final stages of her life-taking illness.

I can understand why a near-death experience can completely change the perspective of a human being in a moment. I also understand these types of life experiences unalterably change one and how they dramatically change your perspective of life in every way. Still, twenty years after the end of this lawsuit, I am still scarred and somewhat disillusioned. I am a street smart kind of guy and no amount of personal success or accolades have ever convinced me that society operates under a benign veil of ignorance. Sadly, life does not always allow honesty and content of character to prevail over racial bias and petty envy.

Still, Lucille and I had chosen to separate ourselves from five generations of comfortable San Luis Valley family history. We moved to Florence and Canon City. We thought our children would have better opportunities to grow up in a climate free of discrimination and racial profiling. Before the lawsuit began, it appeared as though our family had succeeded in these goals. From time to time, however, a negative stereotype or experience would bleed through; reminding us that there were some people who still considered minorities (Mexican/Spanish Americans) to be second-class citizens.

One of these incidents involved my son, Jimmy. Jimmy was always a top-notch student. At one point in time, he became a top spelling bee contender. The local editor of the Florence Weekly Newspaper somehow, for a period of weeks, neglected to include his name and photograph amongst the other contenders that were going to the state finals. Only when my son *won* the Fremont Schools title, did this editor include Jimmy's name and photograph.

Yet, overall, my sons and daughter spent their youth relatively free of the taste of discrimination. They had friends of all races and denominations and our home was a popular hangout for everyone.

It has been said that all politics are local. I've learned, that in small, insular communities, business activities become political. For example, the president of a school board may also decide who gets accepted into the country club or service organizations, who heads up the church building fund and who might sit on the board of directors at the local bank.

Power is either taken or ascribed to and usually only a handful of individuals control a community. Things clearly can get murky and it is in everyone's best interest to act in an above-board manner in all their business transactions. We don't need to look at Fortune 500 Enron scandals to understand what might occur when too much trust and control is vested in one or a few individuals.

My public-mindedness was rewarded by repeated assaults on my character, my friends and my professionalism. My life became a soap opera-a public forum for commentary. Worst of all, I underwent a humiliating and scandalous trial. Everything that I had sought to build in twenty years-my personal fortune, my standing in the community and especially my family's honor was at stake.

What hurt me the most was that many of my friends, including business partners, chose to jump ship. They appeared to hold back, choosing to steer clear of the fray. I felt betrayed. Nonetheless, there were a few who respected my ethics and rallied behind me, such as my good friends, Dr. John and Doris Buglewicz. Though I felt tarnished and betrayed, my shaky faith in the judicial system was ultimately vindicated. However, my faith in my partners, business community and neighbors was lost. It seemed as though everything I had done in my life was of no consequence, and that, to some, I was still an outsider. In the end, I could justifiably walk out of the courtroom with my head held high, cleared of all charges that were brought against me.

Today, when I visit Fremont County (Canon City and Florence), I feel like I'm going home. I don't feel like an expatriate. I've set aside my disappointments and focused on those who have continued to support me in my life. My solace and deep connection is reaffirmed when I am able to visit the gravesites of both my sons and my wife, Lucille.

Taxpayer vs. the IRS

Canon City attorney, William Steinmeyer, called me one Sunday afternoon (mid 1960s) and asked if I would meet him first thing Monday morning. One of his clients was in serious trouble with the Internal Revenue Service (IRS). His client, a doctor, had good reason for concern. I contacted the IRS agent in charge and requested an extension of time to allow for my inspection of the records and prepare for the examination. The agent took all the records to my office so that I could be available to answer his questions. After two weeks of examining the client's records, the agent recommended "no change." In other words, the taxpayer was off the hook. He and his wife were overjoyed. I billed him $1,000.00. This was considered a fairly large fee at the time. Two days later I received a check for $2,500.00. When I attempted to return the difference, he refused it. He said they would be offended if I did not accept the check as written.

A few weeks later the same client took me, as his guest, to a regular meeting of a local service club and introduced me as "his advisor and savior." Shortly thereafter, he proposed my name for membership. A few weeks later, he was informed that the club could "not accept more than one member of the same profession." I was a Certified Public

Accountant and the only other "member of the same profession" was a local bookkeeper. I never attempted to join this club again, though years later other CPAs were accepted into that same club. Eventually, I found a service club (Lions Club) that would accept my membership. A year after being inducted, membership elected me president of the Florence Lions club.

During this same period, I was also elected to the Florence City Council and served two terms as councilman and Mayor-Pro-Tem. While serving on the council, we were able to convince the majority of citizens to approve and fund the building of a new swimming pool for the young people in the community. The only swimming place available had been the Arkansas River nearby and an old pool in Canon City where some Florence people were not welcome. Several young children had drowned in the Arkansas in recent years.

The Chamber Breakfast

Not too long after I opened my accounting practice, I joined the local chamber of commerce. As a new member I wanted to meet new clients, promote my business and make a good impression. I attended every function and participated in any activity sponsored by the chamber. I wanted businessmen to know who I am and what I do.

At that time most of the Colorado state prisons were located in Fremont County, including the women's prison. In fact, this was and still is the major industry in the area.

It so happened that a brand-spanking new prison had just been completed and the whole community was excited because it meant more jobs and more business. This new prison was characterized as "The Escape-Free Prison." Shortly after the facility was opened, the chamber sponsored a 7:00 AM breakfast in the cafeteria of the new prison. Of course, I had to be there.

Everything was going along just fine—the bacon and eggs, potatoes, home made bread and milk—lots of milk because the prison operated a dairy farm. While the speeches and introductions went on, I noticed that one of the inmates paid special attention to me and kept refilling my milk glass.

After a while I looked up and recognized him. It was none other than Alonzo Duran, my grade school classmate from San Antonio.

"What the heck are you doing here?" I asked.

"Just working, what are you doing?" he answered.

"No, I mean why are you here in prison?" He went on to explain he shot a Conejos County deputy sheriff and was sentenced to five years in prison. Fortunately, the deputy didn't die so he was due to get out in three months. A month later I read in the local paper where Alonzo Duran and another inmate had escaped from the "Escape Free Prison", stolen a pickup and wrecked it before they got to Pueblo. Alonzo served another two years after that.

Much to my surprise, my fellow chamber members were favorably impressed. I spent the rest of the meeting explaining how I knew this fine gentleman.

After his release, Alonzo lived the remaining years of his life in the San Luis Valley. He died of natural causes several years later.

By a recent chance conversation with Millie Duran while we both served on the board of directors of a Denver radio station, I learned that Alonzo was her uncle. Almost forty years after the chamber incident, I learned a lot more about this fine gentleman from a close relative.

Millie Duran (*Alonzo's niece*):
I know my uncle had his rough side, but I never was exposed to it. I knew a funny and happy-go-lucky guy. He had a

tremendous amount of respect for my grandmother (Alonzo's mother) and I recognized this even as a very young child.

When I was about 12 years old, he was incarcerated and we corresponded. At that time I learned about another aspect of him that he probably only shared with me. He wrote (from prison)poetry on blue index cards and sent them to me. I would read them but I never discussed them with him. Today, I can't recall anything specific except that he was very optomistic about life.

Alonzo Duran at his parents' home in San Antonio, 1961.

Lessons Learned from My Clients

Perhaps I should say that I gained the best education and the most experience from the "School of Hard Knocks." I can think of several people who I consider to be my mentors (professors) during those school years. Yet, I'm not sure that they're aware of the extent to which they contributed to my business knowledge and financial well being.

I met Everett Cole in the early sixties when I was serving as the auditor for a Royal Gorge area (Canon City) tourist attraction known as Buckskin Joe. He was one of the investors who later became my client. Everett was in his late seventies or early eighties and was crippled by polio. He always drove a new luxury automobile. In spite of his disability, he'd come to my office, on business while his young "friend" waited in the car for him.

Everett had been mayor of Alamosa, Colorado where he owned the theatres and several other businesses. Cole Park was named after Mr. Cole. Everett reminded me of J. Paul Getty, the multimillionaire who made his fortune in the oil business during the depression. Everett owned real estate, theatres, apartments and mines. He even owned a mine in Panama. Every time he visited, he left me with pearls of business advice. He developed an interest in me because he knew of my San Luis Valley background... having come from a poor family.

Everett lived in a Canon City mansion, now the residence of the Dr. Jim and Rita Benzmiller family. His home was full of antiques, paintings and other valuables. He once asked me to keep a box full of gold nuggets and miscellaneous gold pieces while he was away on an extended trip. Why he didn't place these valuables in a safety deposit box, I'll never know. He didn't make a list of the items nor did he ask for a receipt. A couple of months later, he returned and picked up his box.

Another time, he stopped by to discuss a business venture. He'd borrowed several hundred thousand dollars to be repaid over thirty years. I asked how the loan was to be repaid, considering his advanced age. He responded, "Bonney, you never succeed in business, if you're not willing to take a risk. It's even better when it's the bank's money you're risking," he added. I've never forgotten these words.

Ira Macmillan (known as I.A. Macmillan) was a successful realtor and owner of Macmillan Chevrolet, a local auto dealership. Unbeknownst to him, he made a valuable contribution to my business education. Listening to "Mac's" advice and watching him build his business, was an inspiration to me. I met Mac in the early sixties while auditing the financial statements of his auto dealership.

I remember Mac telling me he never borrowed money to invest, unless the loan could be repaid by the investment itself. "Never use your own funds, if you can help it—always use the banks' money," he'd said.

So Lucille and I soon began investing in real estate. In three years, we bought two apartment buildings, a restaurant building, a duplex, a tire store building, several vacant lots and two rental homes... all without using our own funds. Later we got into acquiring repossessed real estate and property tax certificates.

Carl Strunk, another contributor to my business education, and his wife, Jean, owned a small restaurant and fishpond in "East Canon". You could catch your trout in the pond and have it fixed for dinner in the restaurant within a few minutes. This small "mom and pop" restaurant became quite a tourist attraction and expanded to become the largest and finest franchise motel in town.

A former construction worker and boxer, Carl was a self-made entrepreneur, always working on some new venture. Yet, he made time for recreation and was known as a big-game hunter.

It was early December in the late 1960s when Carl asked if I would help him obtain a license to hunt big horn sheep in Mexico. We flew his Piper Cub to Hermosillo, Mexico after spending the night in Nogales, Arizona. The small plane was built to carry four passengers but it was crowded and hot with only two people. On the way up, we nearly crashed, barely missing treetops as we flew over a narrow mountain pass into the San Luis Valley (near the Sand Dunes). I didn't realize how serious it was until Carl explained his concerns on our way back. Of course, we took a different route home.

It was in that crowded cockpit that we spent hours and hours (two days each-way) where Carl shared with me his knowledge and business experience. This was confirmation that I must take one day at a time and live my life to the fullest.

Joe and Earl Berta, owners of Berta Brothers Transportation, became my clients shortly after they acquired a moving company. These hard working brothers were the sons of a highly respected Italian family. Both had worked in the local coal mines. They first started their business when they acquired a truck and a loader and began contracting small dirt-moving jobs. They told me about one of their first jobs away from home. It seems that they had to work long hours to complete the project on time. Joe's wife, Lena and Earl's wife, Carolyn, would travel up to the job site to take them food and other necessities because they were working day and night and slept in their truck.

Their business grew to be one of the largest trucking companies in the state of Colorado. As their accountant, I was their financial advisor. Little did they know that I was taking business classes from them as well.

The Berta brothers taught me that in order to succeed in business, I must be a hard worker, honest, have strong beliefs, be sincere and devoted to my family.

As I have mentioned previously, "Colonel" Fabrizio, one

of my first clients, had a lot of political influence in the state of Colorado.

My desk at the Coors Distributorship was a large double desk, which could be used by two people, one on each side. I sat across from him while working on the company books. I remember the Colonel picking up the phone to call the governor in Denver. In his normal rough voice he said: "Governor, this is the Colonel, in Florence. My nephew is applying for the job of finance director at the state penitentiary. I want you to see that he gets some consideration when the time comes."

Guess what? His nephew got the job a prestigious position at the prison. I believe that the position was second in command to Warden Roy Best. The Colonel never held an elected office, except maybe two or three terms as a city councilman.

After a few months of working for the Colonel, he asked me if I would join the Florence Elks Club. We were both surprised that the local Elks Club did not accept minorities. After I was "blackballed" several times, he told me that it was his brother-in-law who wanted to keep minorities out of the club. I had support from other professionals who'd joined the club after I had been rejected and they joined in an effort to get me in.

Finally one day, the Colonel told me that his brother-in-law was in the hospital and would not be at the meeting on a certain Thursday. I was accepted as a member of the club and initiated the following week. When I was asked to speak,

I said: "Thank you for accepting my membership, but must tell you that this is the first and last meeting I will ever attend." Ever since the doors to the Florence Elks Club have been open to minorities.

This situation was repeated when I tried to join several other organizations and service clubs. One such organization sent me a letter of rejection after the investigating committee had asked if the Pope and the bishop had approved my application. I still have that letter to this day.

The Colonel's words of wisdom on politics included:

- Know the right people.
- Unless you want to run for political office, avoid total commitment to one political party.
- Know which elected officials have your interests in mind.
- Political contributions are okay only if the recipient knows you.
- Remember that your name on a mailing list is not important.
- Contribute to ALL churches as long as you believe their cause is worthy.
- Always stay in the background.
- The less you say, the more influence you have on the process.

There is one more friend and client who taught me valuable lessons in the dealings of big business. I first met Tom (James P. Camerlo) when I was serving on the Florence city council. Tom had petitioned the city to change the water billing rates to his dairy farm located within the city limits. The discussions surrounded the cost per gallon to the city and the reasons why the rates could not be reduced. My contention was that the figures presented by the city manager only included cash expenditures and did not take into consideration the depreciation of the water plant and water lines. If we were to include these costs, water rates would more than double. Tom was an expert lobbyist and so convinced all the council members (except me) to make the rate adjustment.

That same evening, after the meeting, Tom invited me out for a drink at a local restaurant. There he told me about his involvement in a milk co-op headquartered in Colorado Springs. He was a board member of that co-op and asked if I would be interested in rendering certain "Agreed Upon Procedures" for them. The co-op had engaged a national CPA firm to do their annual audit but they were concerned about their internal control. I felt that this was an opportunity to get my foot in the door of a large company so I accepted. The engagement was not only a challenge but it turned out to be a great success and resulted in additional work for my accounting firm.

Later, the Colorado Springs co-op merged with a Denver co-op and grew to become The Mountain Empire Dairymen, Inc. (MEDA). We were given the opportunity to submit a proposal to audit this much larger entity and served as their auditors for approximately eighteen years, until I sold my accounting firm.

I watched Tom grow his dairy business from a few milk cows to one of the largest dairy farms in the country. He currently serves as chairman of the National Milk Producers Federation, headquartered in Arlington, Virginia.

Tom may not know this but I learned a great deal from him. I watched how he dealt with his peers, how he negotiated a business deal and how he used his political savvy to accomplish his goals. What I learned from Tom is stored in my treasury of business acumen.

MY REFLECTIONS

T o some people my life may appear to have consisted of nothing but hardships, illness, deaths and struggles in my profession.

The fact is that my life has been filled with miracles-one miracle after another. Those times when things appeared almost impossible, God was really just performing another miracle in my life. This fact is true for most people, we just don't see, understand nor consider those "drastic changes in our lives", as miracles.

When I reflect now, I realize the first miracle occurred the day I was born. My parents and grandparents began loving me immediately. To be born of poor humble *gente* is something that just does not happen to everyone. To have a grandmother, she lacking a formal education, encourage me to make something of myself—to have a mother who would encourage me to stay in school no matter what—that was a miracle.

My parents made a decision to move out of San Antonio, to Leadville than finally to Alamosa—so that father would have steady work —so that we could be close to good schools. Was this an accident? I don't think so.

In 1948 I graduated from Alamosa High School at age sixteen. Those graduates from well to do families went on to college in various parts of the country. Those graduates from not so wealthy families (mostly my friends) found that the military offered work now and an education later. For me there were no scholarships nor did the military want a sixteen year old. The miracle came from an old man who taught me how to dig a trench for a water line to his home. It took most of the summer but I learned trench digging was not my calling and my grandmother agreed. She loaned me $50. This is the land of opportunity. And I have this going for me.

The Teacher

After two years in college a job opened up in San Antonio, Colorado. An opportunity to teach in a three room (grades K through 8) rural school. The $2,000, before taxes, annual salary was paid within nine months. Now I had a wife, a home in the *two-room dispensita* and a $40 a month car payment. What an experience this was. What I learned here was invaluable years later when, as a CPA, I contracted a consulting job in the country of Honduras. I don't ask nor do I wonder who had his hand in my life. I know the answer.

Career wise, I had a short stint as a caseworker for the Alamosa County Department of Social Services, then back to Adams State College. By this time I knew I wanted to major in Business Administration and work for the FBI. A college buddy of mine had just done that. He wasn't Hispanic, however. Soon after I graduated I discovered that FBI director, J. Edgar Hoover, had a distaste for minorities. So again, a problem becomes "an opportunity in work clothing." I resigned myself to teaching high school business classes. Within three years I get fired, but soon after I become a CPA. Now that's a big miracle.

The Certified Public Accountant

An interesting thing about becoming a CPA in Colorado was that you must have graduated from a college accredited by the Colorado State Board of Accountancy and posses a major in Accounting. Even though Adams State was a legitimate, degree granting Colorado institution, another Colorado institution (the State Board of Accountancy) didn't accredit it. I received an inspiration from up above.

"Get down on your knees, sign up at La Salle Correspondence University, (a school accredited by the Colorado State Board of Accountancy), and take accounting classes at University of Denver on weekends."

I followed the advice and did exactly what I was told. What miracles followed?

- My bookkeeping practice prospered.
- I pass three parts of the CPA exam on my second attempt.
- Six months later I pass the last part (Law) and become a CPA.
- I was now one of the first Hispanic CPAs in Colorado.

My CPA business experienced tremendous growth and expanded throughout the State of Colorado. On more than one occasion, our small local firm competed against national CPA firms and won the client's business. Business opportunities outside my accounting practice seemed to appear from nowhere. Lucille and I dabbled in a few minor business ventures. Then out of the blue came a small real estate investment.

Representatives of the Colorado Society of Certified Public Accountants meet with the Colorado Congressional Delegation in Washington D.C. Spring 1979. (L-R) Bonney Lopez, Congressman Ken Kramer, and Marvin Strait, Colorado Springs CPA.

The Real Estate Venture

L ucille and I were having one of our frequent late evening conversations; and we started wondering why we were not able to grow our savings account. Our income was good but we also had large medical expenses. Our savings account didn't seem to grow higher than $5,000. By now my CPA business had grown to a six-partner firm.

One day an attorney client who owed us $1,500 on a past due accounting fee called me and asked if I would do additional work for his company. He was involved in a large land development project and needed our help. He offered to give us five building lots in payment of the $1,500 past due fee. I talked to my partners but they refused the offer. I then asked Lucille if she would agree to take $1,500 out of our $5,000 savings account, pay the fee and take the five lots in our name. She said okay. Three months later we sold the lots for $15,000. There was no question in our minds that this was a miracle. It had taken years to save $5,000 and three months to make a $13,500 profit. Perhaps we should expand this business, we thought.

The next real estate deal was the sale of a parcel of land to Burger King. We had acquired this property without using our own funds. To minimize the risk, we invited our friends, Dr. John and Doris Buglewicz, to partner with us. We made a nice profit. From then on we continued making the kind of real estate deals you only read about or see advertised on late night television seminar pitches: "Don't use your own funds, put no money down, let the seller finance your purchase, and etc."

Real Estate Tax Certificates

Most of my adult life I've been intrigued with auctions—car auctions, antique auctions, animal auctions, auctioneers—you name it. If there were an auction nearby, I'd be there.

At the beginning, I would just stand there and watch, but if I had a few bucks, I'd buy something. Many were the times when I'd come home from an auction with an old saddle, old books, and a broken down sewing machine or just a box full of junk.

Lucille would say, "Bonney, why do you buy that junk? You know we can't afford it and we always end up taking it to the dump." I knew she was right. Than I remembered hearing that during the great depression many people got wealthy by purchasing the taxes due on real estate. Property owners were so poor they couldn't pay their property taxes so the county treasurer would sell them off at a public sale. I knew this was still happening so I started researching the legal notices in the local newspapers. Before long, there it was, in the paper. "The Fremont County Treasurer will hold the annual tax sale at the county court house on November…"

I took a back seat in this auditorium full of people. I thought to myself "these must be some of those people who got rich during the depression!" Yet, some looked pretty grubby and could have been homeless people. Oh well, they probably don't want others to know they're rich buying the taxes poor people are unable to pay. All bidders are assigned a number. The number appears on a large card which you raise when you bid. My number was #110. Then the bidding starts. I wave at a friend across the room who had just walked in... immediately the auctioneer calls my number "we gottam 45-50 from #110 who'll give me 60-65, we gottam 95 from #325." Now my heart's pumping fast and I'm thinking "What the heck I can go $120." I raise my card again and the auctioneer says "$120 from #110 going once, going twice, sold to #110." *I just bought my first property tax certificate.*

What the heck did I buy? I couldn't even find the property description in the long list of properties being sold. I didn't know if it was the side of a mountain or a swamp. What if it's ten feet of land between two houses? How will I get rid of it? With Lucille's blessings and after the second year, I learned that I really don't have to know much about the property because there's an excellent chance I'll never own it. I will, however, earn interest while my money is invested-anywhere from 14% to 18%—one year as high as 23%—depends on the rates set by the state. Sometimes you do end up owning the property-in such cases the rate of return is much higher, of course.

I started doing this as a hobby about thirty years ago,

now it's a business. I maintain detailed records of all transactions. I even have a line of credit at a local bank for that purpose only. Sometimes I make arrangements for a loan, than take a week or so to travel around to different county tax auctions. Miracle? What else?

Retirement

Lucille's illness was getting progressively worse. Jimmy had received his new kidney from his sister and was back practicing medicine. Mike had just returned from Washington D.C. and was awaiting his appointment to an Executive position at NASW. Ronnie was preparing to enter the police academy. Jilda had just graduated from the University of Denver and started working at a Denver bank.

I was recovering from the stress created by a lawsuit filed against me. Having spent two years dealing with it, a full month in court and a full week on the witness stand, I felt God was telling me it was again time for a change.

After another long evening conversation with Lucille, we decided that I would sell the accounting practice, retire and spend more time with her, at home. By now she had lost her appetite, couldn't do her work around the house and spent a good part of the day resting in bed. I advertised the business in a national publication and within a month I received five offers. I sold the company to a firm from Indiana in June 1984. Of course this was a miracle. God knew Lucille needed me now, more than ever.

After the sale, we spent every moment together. Because

of her loss of appetite, we'd travel to Denver, Colorado Springs and Pueblo in search of food that would agree with her. I tried cooking but… what can I say? Jimmy, Lucille and I once traveled to Corpus Christie, Texas during the month of February. Lucille was cold all the time and she thought that perhaps she'd feel better in a warmer climate. While there, we visited long time friends, Dale and Millie Davidson (Former owners of Davidson-Lindner Chevrolet in Canon City) We also traveled to Mexico City and Mazatlan with John and Doris Buglewicz. And, of course, the trips to the hospitals continued.

One afternoon in late March 1985 we were sitting around the kitchen table and Lucille made the comment, "I guess I'll never get to go to Spain. I've always wanted to go." Next minute I pick up the phone and call Ports of Call in Denver. By 9:00 p.m. that evening we were scheduled on a trip to Spain the first part of May. When she heard that she said "Wouldn't it be nice if we could go with someone we know, like John and Doris?" No sooner said than done. I called John and by next morning they were scheduled on the same trip with us. When we arrived at the airport to leave from Denver, we encountered two other friends taking the same tour, Oliver and Nonie Bolton. Miricale? Of course, who else would have responded to Lucille's desires?

After she died in August 1986, I spent two long lonely years living alone in that large home I had shared with her and my children. I didn't move any of Lucille's things. I just did some remodeling and made landscaping changes, only those things I knew she wanted to have done.

Doing yard work, playing golf, doing maintenance work at the apartments and eating out alone was getting to me-physically, mentally and emotionally. I started visiting my children, Ron, Jim, Mike and Jilda, more often. Mike and Jim's medical conditions were getting worse.

The Tractor Financing Business

For about nine months after my wife died, I tried the trucking business. I formed a wholesale truck dealership; buying and selling used 18-wheeler tractors. I'd buy the tractors in Wisconsin, Minnesota, Nebraska and etc. and sell them to one (retailer) dealer. I knew nothing about the business except that I could make money doing this. The dealer knew the business, could refurbish the tractors and make them look like new. He'd locate the tractor, inspect it to make sure he could make a profit, than call me and suggest a purchase price to me. For example, he'd say

"I located this tractor and I can buy it for $18,000" "I know I can fix it up and sell it for $28,000 to $32,000". I'd say "OK buy it and take title in my name." While I had him on the phone I'd complete the transaction by selling it to him for $22,000.

Within an hour I would wire him the money to pay for the tractor. He'd agree to get it sold within sixty days. If he didn't sell it within that period, he would pay me a floor-planing fee of 2.5% to 3.5% per month on the $22,000 until it was sold.

Why didn't the retail dealer do this on his own and cut me out (the middleman)? First, he couldn't afford to carry the financing and secondly, the banks wouldn't help because of a recent bankruptcy. The venture was very profitable until his market went down the tubes and his profit went with it. I had no choice but to quit at the same time.

The Consulting/Marketing Business

I was spending a lot of time in Denver and in June 1988, I met with my good friend, Pat Comiskey, and told him I was bored and needed something to occupy my mind. I didn't want to work as an accountant but I had many years' experience marketing accounting services for my own firm. I also had a lot of contacts in the Denver area. We shook hands; I formed B. A. Lopez and Associates (a consulting/marketing firm), and began my new profession. Miracle? I was at the right place at the right time.

Micheal, by now the CEO at NASW in Denver, introduced me to most of his political and influential Denver contacts. Within a year, I was serving on an advisory committee to the mayor. Not too long after that I started serving on a couple of committees of the Colorado Contractors Association. Later, I was asked to serve on the Board of Directors of a public (Jazz) radio station, KUVO fm 89.3. This led to membership in the Denver Hispanic Chamber of Commerce, then Mayor Wellington Webb appointed me to the Board of Trustees of the Denver Employees Retirement Plan (DERP). I'm currently serving as chairman of the board.

Why was it so important that I join and become active in so many organizations? Because I knew that the best way to market a CPA firm was to become well known in the community where you want to market your services. I had over thirty years experience doing this very same thing for my own firm—much of the time when it was supposedly "unethical" and against the rules of the profession. During my early years in the accounting business, twice I was called before the licensing board. I was questioned about two things: 1) listing my name in the yellow pages phone directories in Pueblo and Canon City and 2) allowing a remodeling company to photograph and use the picture of the inside of my office in one of their company ads.

I disagreed with the board but I apologized and they left me alone. The "advertising and ethics" rules seemed to apply only to small firms because large national firms always found ways to market their services. Thank God things have changed. Now those large firms are having to deal with their own, more serious "ethics" problems.

The consulting part of the business primarily consists of consulting on governmental engagements. The marketing part requires ninety percent of the effort. I devote time to contacting potential new clients, arranging meetings between our professional staff and the new clients, try to match expertise and personality between staff and client, prepare written proposals for presentation to prospective clients, design new marketing materials and etc.

Recent Business and Pleasure Travels

I n April 1999 I traveled to Asia as a representative of the Denver Employees Retirement Plan (DERP). The trip was sponsored by an organization known as "Pensions 2000". This organization arranges one or two business trips a year for board members and executives of U.S. and Canadian employee pension plans. Most of the trips are to places outside the United States where the pension entities have or intend to make international investments.

Conference at the Shilla Hotel in Seoul, Korea. Speaker: Kim Dao-Jung, President of South Korea. Bonney seated in second row, third person from the right, April 1999.

Kim Dae-jung, President of the Republic of South Korea speaking at the conference at the Shilla Hotel, April 1999.

This particular trip was to South Korea, Taiwan and Hong Kong. The group consisted of approximately 120 representatives from various public and non-public pension plans. On arrival, we were greeted by persons in high positions and treated like royalty in each place we visited.

The President of South Korea, bank presidents and ambassadors made formal presentations to the group. CEOs of major companies as well

"Politicos" interested in foreign investments also spoke to the group. It was not all work, however. Afternoons and evenings we were entertained by the best and we visited places we only read about, such as the DMZ (Demilitarized Zone) between North and South Korea.

Nobel Peace Prize winner, 74 year old South Korean President Kim Dae-jung, impressed me the most. Perhaps because I had read about this dissident-turned-president and heard that he had been imprisoned because of his political beliefs, I looked forward to meeting him.

We were told that President Kim had been tortured

while in a communist prison. We noticed he appeared to limp when he walked. He was also heavily guarded and spoke from a bulletproof podium.

I must say I am proud to have met this great statesman who capped his policy of engaging the communist north by attending an historic summit in the North Korean capital Pyongyang with North Korean leader Kim Jong-Il.

Later the same year (October 1999) I visited Spain for the third time. This time as a guest of my Alamosa High School buddy, now Ambassador Edward L. Romero.

The past few years, I've had the opportunity to visit England, Hawaii, France, the Bahamas, Germany, Jamaica, Holland and Switzerland. In June 2001 we toured Italy and Sicily for three and a half weeks. The week of September 11, 2001 we were scheduled to attend conferences in Athens Greece and Istanbul Turkey, however, the conference was cancelled due to the terrorist attack in New York City. Miracle? A San Antonio pea picker has been given the opportunity to travel abroad and meet distinguished people.

Bonney attempting to keep the Leaning Tower of Pisa from tipping over, June 2001.

Para mis Hijos
y mis Nietos

Ronald, Jilda, Joelle, Gabriel, Joshua and Jennifer

This is my story as I remember it and as I believe Lucille, Micheal and Jimmy would have wanted it related to you. I must say that this is only a small glimpse of the story and there is a lot more to be recorded. God willing, we will be given the time, health and energy to record the rest of the story.

Remember that only the form of anything, not the substance ever really changes. Our bodies, our homes, our automobiles and our wealth are made to deteriorate or eventually die and crumble. That which remains, the memories of our loved ones, is most important.

As long as we pass our stories down to our sons and our daughters, repeating the names of *la gente*, the people with whom we have shared our lives will live forever.

MICHEAL'S CHILDREN

Joelle Lopez, business major,
Bachelor of Science degree,
University of Colorado, 2002.

Gabriel Lopez, junior at
Colorado State University
majoring in pre-law.

RONALD'S CHILDREN

Joshua Lopez, sophomore at
St. Mary's High School in
Colorado Springs.

Jennifer Lopez, seventh
grade at Divine Redeemer
Catholic School in
Colorado Springs.